Paths *to* Prayer

Pat Fosarelli's book is to the spiritual life what a good map is to the traveler: a look at the big picture that allows pilgrims to know something of the terrain they will traverse. More specifically, she shows us not only the paths, but also those who forged them: saints and mystics whose thirst for God drove them, under the gentle but insistent voice of God, into previously unexplored places. She shows us how their journeys toward deeper and broader love of God have opened for us many avenues of growth in faith, hope, and love.

Tim Muldoon
Author of *The Ignatian Workout*

Paths *to* Prayer

A Field Guide
to *Ten Catholic Traditions*

PAT FOSARELLI

ave maria press **AmP** notre dame, indiana

Founded in 1865, Ave Maria Press is a ministry of the Indiana Province of Holy Cross.

www.avemariapress.com

ISBN-10 1-59471-218-2   ISBN-13 978-1-59471-218-0

Cover and text design by Brian C. Conley

Printed and bound in the United States of America.
Library of Congress Cataloging-in-Publication Data is available.

Contents

Introduction

When I was younger, I thought that there was one spirituality for Catholics and another spirituality for everyone else. Imagine my surprise in graduate school when I realized that there were many, many traditions of Catholic spirituality! Although these traditions share some commonalities, they are different because their founders were different and they were developed at different times and places in history.

Because of space limitation, this book will explore only the *major* schools of Catholic spirituality. These spiritual traditions will generally be presented in their chronological order of appearance in history, except when a tradition and its reformation are important to keep together. The traditions that will be explored include Augustinian, Benedictine, Cistercian (or Trappist), Dominican, Franciscan, Carmelite, Ignatian, Salesian, Mystical, and twentieth-century Lay Spirituality.

These spiritual traditions are considered *major* because, over time, they have had influence far beyond both their founders and their earliest followers. In many ways, they are timeless. Any one of these traditions could merit an entire book of its own, describing, in depth, the founder, the times in which he or she lived, and the hallmarks of each spiritual tradition.

This book, however, is designed to be an overview of these traditions. It is a book meant to acquaint readers with what these major traditions of spirituality cherish so that readers might explore the traditions on their own. Think of this book as a field guide to the traditions, helping readers to become acquainted with each one.

Each chapter will explore the hallmarks of a particular tradition. This is important because while there are essential commonalities in each spirituality (they are, after all, part of the Catholic tradition), there are certainly differences. Founders of the great traditions came from different historical periods. They had different interests and were affected by the events of their times, both religious and secular. For each of these traditions, therefore, a few words need to be said in each chapter about the founder and the cultural milieu that inspired his or her tradition.

Examples of important works by the founder or by a prominent member of the tradition will be provided to help facilitate readers' exploration of the tradition in greater detail at a later time. At certain points, words from the founder or a prominent member of the community will be included so as to give readers the opportunity to learn, in the founder's or members' own words, exactly what they were seeking. That is so important for our understanding of their devotion! Even though many of the quoted words are translations and things can be lost or gained in translation, it *is* helpful to hear others' own words on what their goals were.

There are certainly other schools of Catholic spirituality, other traditions that will not be mentioned here. This is a book that is meant to get readers started, so that, having a better understanding of some of the major Catholic spiritual traditions, readers can then move on to traditions they might like to explore.

A personal note to each reader: do not be the least bit surprised if you resonate with one particular school or tradition and not at all with another. This is very common. It will almost seem as if one particular founder knows something about your life and is speaking directly to you, while another founder leaves you cold. That is why multiple spiritualities are presented—so that you, the reader, can decide what works for you. Because God touches individuals in different ways, in the end, all of these traditions are worthwhile because all of them can lead to God.

In this introduction, I would like to pose two questions. One, what is the purpose of a spiritual tradition? Two, why in the world are there so many different ones? The first question is fairly easy to answer. The purpose of a spiritual tradition is to provide a means for someone to draw closer to God. A tradition provides rules and guidelines for how one might approach God from that tradition's perspective. Many of us need structure. We can't simply pick one spiritual practice from here and another from there—it just doesn't gel for us. Traditions represent a kind of "package deal." As such, you may find that not every feature in a tradition will fit you, even if many of the features *do* resonate with you

Moving on to the second question, we have already mentioned that the founders came from very different times and places. A student of mine once remarked: "Why didn't the founders simply do a 'tweaking' of a tradition that was already there? Why did they have to invent something new, especially when there are commonalities?"

All of the founders truly believed that they were responding to a personal call from God, and that they were doing what God wanted them to do. Although the founders might have adapted some aspects from a previous spiritual tradition, they had a slightly different spin on things. In embracing that spin, they were much better able to craft what they felt God was calling them to do.

Frequently, a tradition is the result of some political or church-related upheaval, and the founder was trying to work with those events in his or her life and in the lives of others. In addition, founders differed in temperament. Some were quiet, wanting to be alone in solitude, while others were far more gregarious, wanting groups of people around them, and wanting to go out beyond the walls of a monastery or church, in order to be with the people who lived outside those walls.

In spite of these differences, each tradition shares certain commonalities. First, each tradition focuses on God because God is the source of all there is. The tradition may describe God in unique language, but it is all God-focused. Second, the love of God is emphasized in each of these traditions. We are called to love God. We are called to be grateful to God for what God has done for us. In loving

God, we become our more authentic selves, and many of the traditions actually say this overtly. This is important, for who does not wish to be authentic?

Third, each tradition emphasizes devotion to Christ and imitation of him. This is stated in a number of ways, but the idea is that Christ became one of us, and in becoming one of us, he knew the pain, joy, friendships, betrayal, and fatigue of the human condition. He knew what we know, and he shares our experience. Because he shares our experience, we can imitate him. To be sure, we will not imitate him perfectly, because we are imperfect creatures. But we are always called to imitate Christ, especially in his regard for others, and in his dedication to his *Abba*.

Lastly, a commonality that all traditions share is service to others. Each founder believed that we see Christ in other people. For that reason, serving others was the same as serving Christ. In addition, others are members of God's family—as beloved as we are.

Let me give you some examples of how this works. We can express our love of God through prayers, but there are certainly different forms of prayer, just as there are different images of God. Some people like to pray silently, while some people like to pray aloud. Some people like to pray in solitude, while others like to pray in community. In terms of different images of God, some people think of God, first and foremost, as their friend. On the other hand, others immediately think of a majestic God, the creator of all that is, and not someone we can just "buddy up to." Naturally, this means that there will be different forms of prayer and different ways of expressing our love for God.

As another example, we can express our devotion and imitation of Christ by the way we live. Some people like to imitate Christ's solitude. In gospel accounts, Christ went away to be alone. He did this to enter into prayer and communication with his Abba. That is how some people prefer to imitate Christ. Other individuals feel that it is better to imitate the earthly Christ in the way he was most frequently experienced, surrounded by his disciples and by people who needed him. Such individuals want to be immersed in the world. They feel that it would not be authentic for them to be in solitude, whether in the wilderness or in their room.

We can express our service to others in a myriad of ways. Some may be born preachers or teachers, while others see themselves as serving the ill or the poor in hospices, in soup kitchens, wherever those individuals are found. The most important thing that any of us who believe in God can do is to live out our beliefs in a way that is most keeping with who we are. This was true in the fourth century, the sixteenth century, *and* today.

Most of us have neither the ability nor desire to enter a monastery. Most of us live in community with our own families. When we live in a community, especially the community of family, we learn very quickly that our own needs do not always take precedence. We learn that others' needs must frequently come before our own. Some of the traditions are known for sending members to foreign mission fields, and that might not be at all realistic for many of us. But we can certainly serve in our own families, churches, and communities. There is great need all around us. We do not need to go six thousand miles away. Sometimes we only need to go six blocks away. We can't all leave the secular world to find God in the desert or the monastery. But we can all find God in the details of our lives, because if we believe that God created all things, then God is there in the details as well as in the big things.

Perhaps you are thinking, "What do people who lived a thousand or more years ago have to say to us today?" Life is so different now than it was then. We can communicate with others who live across the globe in seconds. We can know what is happening in a place halfway around the world within moments, whereas in previous times, it would have taken people months to acquire that information, if they ever learned at all. I believe that certain people of a thousand or more years ago, especially those who were thinking a great deal about human nature, have quite a lot to say to us. Human nature does not change, and the ways to approach God do not change. We have our own problems, to be sure. We have our own challenges. But that does not mean the basics of human nature are different. All of us have goals. All of us face disappointments. All of us face tragedy at some point in our lives. All of us experience joys. Spiritual traditions work with the stuff of lives—real lives—and try to use that stuff in order to move individuals more closely to God.

I would like to close this introduction with a prayer that the founder of the Jesuits, St. Ignatius of Loyola, used to begin his *Spiritual Exercises*. He did not invent the prayer—the prayer was in use before he adapted it—but it is a good way to begin the journey that this book represents. It is called the *anima Christi*, which is Latin for "Soul of Christ" (Puhl xvii).

> Soul of Christ, sanctify me
> Body of Christ, save me
> Blood of Christ, inebriate me
> Water from the side of Christ, wash me,
> Passion of Christ, strengthen me,
> Oh, good Jesus, hear me,
> Within Thy wounds, hide me,
> Permit me not to be separated from Thee,
> From the wicked foe, defend me,
> At the hour of my death, call me,
> And bid me come to Thee,
> That with Thy saints,
> I may praise Thee, forever and ever,
>
> Amen.

References

Puhl, Louis. *The Spiritual Exercises of St. Ignatius: Based on Studies in the Language of the Autograph*. Chicago: Loyola Press, 1951.

one

Augustinian Spirituality

Augustine and His World

The man we know as St. Augustine was born in the year 354 to Monica, a Christian, and Patricius, a pagan, in Thagaste, North Africa (modern-day Algeria). Monica and Patricius were respected members of Roman society, having some social and political connections. This made it possible for Augustine to have an excellent education, in which he excelled.

By the time of Augustine's birth, Christianity was no longer a persecuted religion. Unlike Christians who had come before her, Monica was free to practice her religion publicly and, according to Augustine in his autobiography *Confessions*, she was very pious. But the young Augustine would have none of it. By his own honest account, he was a wayward youth, enjoying many sensual pleasures. He ran with a wild crowd, stealing when he had no need to do so, and getting involved in multiple sexual liaisons, one of which culminated in having a son outside of marriage.

Augustine studied the major religious and philosophical views of his time. At one point he became a member of the Manichees, a group with beliefs drawn from various belief systems, including Christianity. Among other beliefs, the Manichees believed that good and evil were equal forces, engaged in a cosmic struggle. Eventually, Augustine became disillusioned with the Manichees.

He went to Milan, Italy, to take a teaching position, and there he opened his own school. Always intellectually curious, Augustine began to attend Bishop Ambrose's sermons. Ambrose of Milan, an eloquent and gifted speaker, gave the young Augustine much to consider. Soon Augustine began to read the New Testament, especially the letters of Paul, hoping both to understand them better and to see what guidance they might provide for his own life. But despite these efforts, he remained confused and dejected, and his desire for wisdom and peace—both psychological and spiritual—eluded him.

One day, Augustine was sitting in a friend's garden, wondering just how long it was going to take him to become close to God. He wondered why the God who was presented in his training seemed far from Augustine, his friends, and his world. In frustration, he wept. Then, something unexpected happened. This is his own account of conversion to Christ:

> I was asking myself these questions, weeping all the while with the most bitter sorrow in my heart, when all at once I heard the sing-song voice of a child in a nearby house. Whether it was the voice of a boy or girl, I cannot say, but again and again it repeated the refrain, "Take it and read; take it and read." At this, I looked up, thinking hard whether there was any kind of game in which children used to chant words like these, but I could not remember hearing them before. I stemmed my flood of tears and stood up, telling myself that this could only be a divine command to open my book of Scripture and read the first passage on which my eyes should fall. . . . So I hurried back to the place where Alypius [his friend] was sitting, for when I stood up to move away I had put down the book containing Paul's epistles. I seized it and opened it, and in silence I read the first passage on which my eyes fell: "Not in revelling and drunkenness, not in lust and

wantonness, not in quarrels and rivalries. Rather, arm yourselves with the Lord Jesus Christ; spend no more thought on nature and nature's appetites." For in an instance, as I came to the end of the sentence, it was as though the light of confidence flooded into my heart and all darkness of doubt was dispelled. (*Confessions*, 8:12, 177–78)

The passage that Augustine encountered was Romans 13:13–14, and in modern translation it reads: "Let us conduct ourselves properly as in the day, not in orgies and drunkenness, not in promiscuity and licentiousness, not in rivalry or jealously. But put on the Lord Jesus Christ and make no provisions for the desires of the flesh."

Reflecting on his life, Augustine believed that the passage was speaking directly to him, and from that day forward, he dedicated his life to Christ. He was instructed in the Christian faith and was baptized in 387. He lived several years as a lay ascetic, living in community with other like-minded individuals, with whom he prayed and, with the aid of grace, sought to conquer his passions. Augustine was ordained to the priesthood in 391, and in the year 395, almost against his will, he was named the bishop of Hippo in Africa.

Bishop Augustine lived another thirty-five years, discussing the faith with believers, debating the faith with non-believers, settling difficult controversies, and acting as pastor for his community. He lived long enough to see the world he knew decimated by invading barbarian tribes coming from the east and north: Huns, Vandals, and Visigoths. The Goths had sacked Rome in 410, and the Vandals had marched on Carthage as Augustine lay dying. The world in which Augustine had developed his spirituality would radically change after his death (in 430), especially with the fall of the western Roman Empire in 476. Yet, Augustine's words did not die with him; indeed, his ideas formed the foundations of Western Christianity.

Augustine's writings are a magnificent legacy for those who came after him. A prolific writer, Augustine was a tireless champion of Christianity, and he wrote many treatises against both paganism and the various heresies of his time. In addition, he wrote numerous sermons, many of which still exist today. His books include the aforementioned *Confessions* and *The City of God*, a work that compares and contrasts the heavenly kingdom with earthly ones, most notably that of imperial Rome.

Augustine is called the Doctor of Grace, a title given because so many of his writings and sermons focused on grace as God's free gift to us. For Augustine, everything that anyone has is a gift from God. We did not create ourselves, we did not redeem ourselves, and we do not sanctify ourselves. It is God's work always. Augustine humbly recognized that, without God's help (or grace), no human being could do anything—especially that which is good—on his or her own. Augustine was ever grateful for the gift of grace and encouraged those whom he pastored to be grateful as well, accepting grace from God and cooperating with the gift in the way that he or she was capable.

Two quotations from his autobiography *Confessions* underscore Augustine's absolute conviction that he could not save himself. The first is Augustine's utter confusion about why sin had such an attraction for him. He wrote:

> I was willing to steal, and steal I did, although I was not compelled by any lack, unless it were the lack of a sense of justice or a distaste for what was right, and a greedy love of doing wrong. For of what I stole, I already had plenty, and much better at that, and I had no wish to enjoy the things I coveted by stealing, but only to enjoy the theft itself and the sin. There was a pear tree near our vineyard, loaded with fruit that was attractive neither to look at nor to taste. Late one night, a band of ruffians, myself included, went off to shake down the fruit and carry it away, for we continued our games out of doors until well after dark, as was our pernicious habit. We took away an enormous quantity

of pears, not to eat them ourselves, but simply to throw them down to the pigs. Perhaps we ate some of them, but our real pleasure consisted in doing something that was forbidden. Look into my heart, O God . . . Let my heart now tell you what prompted me to do wrong for no purpose, and why it was only my own love of mischief that made me do it. The evil in me was foul, but I loved it. I loved my own perdition and my own faults, not the things for which I committed wrong but the wrong itself. (II:4, 47–8) . . . But it was not the pears that my unhappy soul desired. I had plenty of my own, better than those, and I only picked them so that I might steal. For no sooner had I picked them than I threw them away, and tasted nothing in them, but my own sin, which I relished and enjoyed, If any part of one of those pears passed my lips, it was the sin that gave it flavor. (II:6, 49)

The second quotation is an expression of Augustine's dismay that it took him as long as it did to come to God, given all that God had done for him. Augustine acknowledged that, in the end, it took God's initiative and aid for him to come to God at all. His sadness at his delayed conversion to God would be more than compensated by the closeness to God he would eventually experience. Augustine wrote:

I have learned to love you late, Beauty at once so ancient and so new! I have learned to love you late! You were within me, and I was in the world outside myself. I searched for you outside myself and, disfigured as I was, I fell upon the lovely things of your creation. You were with me, but I was not with you. The beautiful things of this world kept me far from you and yet, if they had not been in you, they would have no being at all. You called me; you cried aloud to me; you broke my barriers

of defenses. You shone upon me; your radiance en-
veloped me; you put my blindness to flight. You
shed your fragrance about me; I drew breath and
now I gasp for your sweet odor. I tasted you, and
now I hunger and thirst for you. You touched me,
and I am inflamed with love of your peace. (10:27;
231–32)

Hallmarks of Augustinian Spirituality

Augustinian spirituality is deeply Trinitarian. Augustine's
conception of who God is and how God works in our lives is
deeply affected by his understanding of God as Father, Son,
and Holy Spirit.

In his book *On the Trinity,* Augustine discussed one of the most
challenging Christian doctrines. The doctrine of the Trinity—one
God in three Persons—is challenging to understand because we
think of "person" as a discrete entity and do not experience persons as a unity. Yet, the Trinity demonstrates the nature and extent
of God's love.

God created everything that is seen and unseen. In the beginning, it was all good, because God is good. After sin entered the
world, Jesus Christ came to restore human beings to proper relationship with God. While on earth, Jesus revealed God the Father
through his words and actions, especially his passion and death on
the cross. After his resurrection, Jesus sent the Holy Spirit to be ev-
ermore with humanity, shaping us into persons who are in right relationship with God.

Through all these actions, God is known by us as self-giving
love, a Being who desires relationship with all creatures. Recognizing the power of God's love, Christians are baptized with what is
called a Trinitarian formula ("In the name of the Father, and of the
Son, and of the Holy Spirit"). The Trinity is all about relationship—
each Person to one another, and to all creation. Since the Trinity
is one through mutual love, and since human beings are joined to
Christ in baptism, Christians are joined to the Trinity through God's

grace, which is love. This grace permits us to draw closer to God in love. Grace transforms us in that the more we love God, the more we wish to do God's will; the more we wish to do God's will, the more we love God, one another, and creation, in imitation of God.

Christian faith teaches that the goal of human life is to become such a lover of God, one another, and all creation, that human life becomes an authentic image of the self-giving love of the Trinity. In accepting the gift of God's love, we accept the challenge of becoming more like God.

Augustinian spirituality is Christocentric. Augustine's spiritual vision is grounded in the life and work of Jesus Christ. It is through Jesus that we are welcomed into the Trinitarian love life.

From the time of his conversion, Augustine sought to join himself to Christ, who became the center of his life, his alpha and omega. Christ is the Word, the Healer, and the "least of these" (Mt 25), and he is always in union with his members in the body of Christ, as St. Paul noted in 1 Corinthians.

Because of his own struggles with sin, Augustine understood that human beings needed to be healed before they could be joined to God as Trinity, and that this was simply not something they could do on their own. They needed to be healed by Christ, whom Augustine considered to be not only our mediator (since he was both human and divine) but also our physician. Christ would not force healing upon us but would, instead, wait for us to acknowledge our need for healing and forgiveness. After making this acknowledgment, we prepare ourselves for healing through prayer, the reading of scripture, and fasting. These activities are disciplines that take the focus of our minds away from ourselves and place the focus on God. Once Christ's healing is underway, we become filled with gratitude for what God has done for us. Only then can we truly love as God desires.

Not only is Christ our physician who heals us, but he is also our teacher, instructing us on how to live by his words and by his example, as recorded in scripture. In order to learn well from Christ, we must humbly acknowledge our ignorance and our weakness. Augustine felt that Christ's life is our life. For Augustine, the incarnation showed God's great love for us. By becoming one with us as a human being, God showed his solidarity with humanity. By sharing himself with humanity, Christ showed the depths of his love for the human race, and, as such, he is our supreme example of what it means to love.

Augustinian spirituality seeks growth in true wisdom.

Augustine sought wisdom his entire life. For Augustine, wisdom is not just intelligence. It is God's gift to human beings. But we must eagerly search for it and be prepared for it in order to accept it properly. Again, that occurs through reading scripture, praying, and fasting. Through these activities, we adopt a reverence and awe toward God and better understand how our own sinfulness moves us away from that God. This understanding brings both humility and sadness about our lives, which, in turn, make us eager to become right with God. We begin to understand that only God can save us; we cannot save ourselves. This is Augustine's message about grace. Instead of focusing on what's in it for us, we focus on God and do actions out of love for God and not for our own schemes and projects. True wisdom always results in loving actions, mirroring God's love that led to creation and Christ's love for sinful humanity that led to his death on the cross.

The more we love, the more we are united to God and the wiser we become, because we become more like God. Becoming more like God means that, in the end, we become more authentic, freer to choose good rather than evil. Augustine firmly believed that one's inner self was the most authentic self because God lived in one's heart. The more we can believe that God is at the center of our identity, the more we can be what God created us to be. God's gift of grace enables all this to occur. But this gift is not forced upon us. We must accept it and then respond to it in love.

Augustinian spirituality is ultimately all about love.

Augustine believed that scripture is the story of God's love for humankind. When he preached or wrote about a passage from scripture, he often used language about the heart to underscore the importance of love, for the heart was felt to be the place in which love originated. Our greatest love is to be directed to God who is love.

God's grace permits us to assent to love—love of God and love of our neighbor. The initiative is God's and not ours. God calls, and we respond. As we respond to this call and grow in love of God, God's desire becomes our own, and we begin to treat others as Christ treated others. Such a transformation does not occur suddenly or quickly. It comes bit by bit, as we sometimes take two steps forward and three steps backward. Receiving the sacraments, especially the eucharist and reconciliation, facilitates our spiritual growth. As a good pastor, Augustine recognized the need for frequent reception of the eucharist in order to remain joined to Christ.

This union with Christ is contemplation. Although many people think of contemplation as something only "mystics" do, that type of thought is erroneous. When he lived on this earth, Christ was in union with the Father and the Spirit. Yet he went about teaching, preaching, and serving others, all in great humility. Because Christ is our model for what a human life of humility, integrity, and union with God looks like, we are to serve joyfully in the way that God has empowered us to do. This is what true love looks like.

Augustinian Community Rule

Augustine founded communities in which men could live their lives in the world, but still grow in their union with Christ. He did not believe that monks or priests should be apart from the world but immersed in it, bearing witness to their fidelity to Christ and their desire to serve others as Christ served us. Stated another way, words and actions had to match.

Naturally, these communities of men focused on God, but they also focused on loving and serving other human beings. Service had to be done with compassion and love, or it was not true service at all. Augustinian communities served the Church through their defense of the Church laws and traditions, and the papacy throughout the ages.

Most likely influenced by earlier desert monastic traditions, Augustine offered a brief rule of living for those in community. It focused on what monks needed to practice in order to live in a community of love. In terms of the monks' service to each other, each man in community had to learn to deny himself for the sake of others and to share communal resources. He had to learn to be prayerful, moderate, and chaste. He had to learn how to seek forgiveness, to forgive, and to correct his fellow monks, all for the good of the community. All of this was to be done in the name of humility and love (Martin 59).

True to Augustine's own keen intellect, he did not wish to exclude the intellectual aspect of the human person, for he believed that our intellects are made in the image and likeness of God. For that reason, he encouraged those in his communities to think, read, study, speak, and even debate with one another so that learning and understanding might flourish. These spiritual practices or disciplines are good ones for any Christian to embrace, whether or not they are Augustinian.

Well-Known Augustinians

Desiderius Erasmus (1466–1536): Dutch humanist. In 1516, Erasmus published a highly annotated Greek version of the New Testament accompanied by a classical Latin text to replace the widely used Vulgate version written by St. Jerome.

Martin Luther (1483–1546): Protestant reformer. Luther was an Augustinian monk who believed that his reforms would bring the Roman Church back to its roots.

Gregor Mendel (1822–1884): Father of modern genetics. Mendel was an Augustinian monk when he did his famous experiments on pea plants.

References for Learning More about Augustinian Spirituality

Augustine. *Confessions*. Trans. R.S. Pine-Coffin. New York: Penguin Classics, 1961.

Clark, Mary. "Augustinian Spirituality" in Michael Downey, ed. *The New Dictionary of Catholic Spirituality*. Collegeville, MN: Liturgical Press, 1993.

Martin, Thomas. "Augustinian Spirituality" in Stephen Costello, ed. *The Search for Spirituality: Seven Paths within the Catholic Tradition*. Dublin: Liffey Press, 2002.

_____. *Our Restless Heart: The Augustinian Tradition*. Maryknoll, NY: Orbis Books, 2003.

Benedictine Spirituality

Benedict and His World

Benedict of Nursia, generally regarded as the father of Western monasticism, lived from 480 to 550. As he did not write anything about himself, most of what we know about him is second-hand. The main source of information about Benedict's life comes from Pope Gregory the Great, who wrote about Benedict fifty years or so after his death.

Benedict and his twin sister Scholastica were raised in privileged circumstances in Nursia, northeast of Rome. Because Benedict showed intellectual promise, he was sent to Rome to study. He was deeply disturbed by the overt sinfulness he saw all around him in Rome. To protect himself from the excesses of Roman life, he fled to a desolate area, where he lived alone in a cave for three years. There, he attempted to learn more about God and how to better serve him. Although today we might think that such behavior is strange, the people of Benedict's time recognized it as holiness.

Soon, other young men approached him, wishing to join him in community. After one failed attempt to establish a religious community of men, Benedict successfully founded a community at Subiaco, Italy. Eventually, however, he left the community due to internal strife. Struggling to find men who were committed to holiness and who wanted to live the holy yet undeniably austere life upon which he insisted, he eventually founded a community that not only would survive but also become renowned, at Monte Cassino, close to Naples.

Benedict understood that whenever human beings live together, they are capable of misunderstanding one another. The greater the variety of personality types which exist together, the more likely that misunderstandings arise. For that reason, Benedict developed a Rule for community living, which was drawn largely from the rules of older monastic orders. Benedict's Rule helped facilitate relationships among the very diverse members of his young community: recent converts to Christianity, long-time Christians, illiterate men, highly educated men, and so on. The ultimate goal of the Rule was to facilitate a communal life that was holy but moderate and practical. The men in such a community would live well-balanced lives of prayer, work, solitude, and community.

Benedict's Rule has been used by those seeking spiritual growth from his time to our own. However, as with most religious orders, the various monasteries founded on his Rule grew somewhat lax in their observance in the years following Benedict's death. This, in turn, led to various reform movements. For example, Benedict of Aniane (750–821), a former member of Charlemagne's court, had the Emperor's support to not only return to the rigor of the original Benedictine Rule, but also to unify other orders' rules under the Rule of Benedict. Yet even these reforms were not sufficient to satisfy those who wanted a life of deep austerity. Over the centuries, reformers intent on living the original Benedictine ideal would continue to emerge. The Cistercian reform was especially significant and is given its own chapter in this volume.

Hallmarks of Benedictine Spirituality

Benedictine spirituality is one that seeks God and recognizes God's presence in all things, activities, and relationships.

Benedict believed that God was far more than human beings could ever imagine in terms of majesty, knowledge, power, mercy, and love. While the fullness of these qualities is beyond human comprehension, they can be recognized in creation. Benedict believed that we can learn about God by respectfully acknowledging all created beings and objects that we encounter, all of which God willed to exist. For Benedict, not only was God's creative genius present in creation, but also God's great love. Hence, Benedict believed that the appropriate response to creation was humble awe. We must keep in mind that, for Benedict, awe was not equivalent to fear. Rather, awe was a profound respect that flowed out of love. The more we understand about God in his creation, the more we love God, and the more we love God, the more awestruck we are by God's being.

Benedictine spirituality seeks and sees Christ in others.

Benedict was very moved by the twenty-fifth chapter of the Gospel of Matthew. In this chapter, commonly known as the Last Judgment, the king rewards those who fed the hungry, gave drink to the thirsty, welcomed the stranger, clothed the naked, cared for the ill, and visited the imprisoned. The king tells those rewarded that they were doing these things for the king himself. Those being rewarded are amazed because they could never recall seeing the king. The king responds, "Whenever you did it to the least of these, you did it to me." These were galvanizing words for Benedict, who realized that Christ was present in each person, regardless of their station in life. For that reason, we are to treat others in the manner that we would treat Christ, for this is, indeed, the way we manifest our love for him.

Benedictine spirituality leads to supporting others, especially in community.

Individuals in Benedict's community were to work, pray, and take meals together. The image of a community life that balances work, prayer, and meals is especially poignant today, because we are frequently so scattered. Even persons who do not live formally "in community" are called by God to serve and support those around them in committed, appropriate ways. We *all* live in community, whether in our families, our neighborhoods, or our parishes, and we do well to regard those around us with respect and render loving service to them.

Benedictine spirituality responds to God through public prayer, individual spiritual reading, and manual labor.

God is Lord of all aspects of an individual's life; there is no place from which God is excluded. For that reason, one who espouses the Benedictine way of life recognizes that God can always be found, if one truly wishes to look. Furthermore, given that God always makes the first move toward his creatures, a creature responds to God in everyday activities. Our basic response to God's initiative, whether or not we live in a monastery, is prayer and work.

Benedictine spirituality emphasizes humility and obedience.

Christ humbled himself in becoming human; his living conditions while on earth were certainly humble. Christ's followers are called to imitate this humility. But humility is not only external, but internal as well, and that is where obedience comes in. We are to obey those who have lawful authority over us, even if it seems that they know less than we do. This is a hard lesson for monks to learn as they cultivate a relationship with their abbot, and it is no easier for us, as the prevailing culture encourages us to question authority always.

Benedictine spirituality emphasizes asceticism and poverty.

Christ was poor. His followers are called to be the same. Like humility, poverty is not only external, but internal. Choosing to be poor as Christ was poor does not mean living a life of miserable destitution, but it does mean that we realize that everything we are and everything we have has been given to us by God. We have neither made ourselves nor given ourselves our talents. Profound gratitude for all we have been given is the first step toward authentic Christian poverty. Cultivating an external poverty is important to Benedictine spirituality, as well. Those in Benedict's community were true ascetics, having little and needing less. This is a good message for us today, we who have so much that we do not need. We are called to quiet the inner voices that claim we need more and become grateful for having "just enough," thanking God and eagerly sharing what we have been freely given.

Benedictine spirituality encourages discernment.

Those who lived in Benedictine communities had individual conferences with a superior who would assist them in their spiritual growth and difficulties. For a long time, it was widely believed that only the ordained or vowed religious needed spiritual guides or directors, but in the late twentieth century, there came the recognition that anyone can benefit from the assistance of another person who is wiser in spiritual matters and can offer an objective opinion as to whether one is being either too easy or too hard on oneself. This recognition of the need for discernment makes Benedictine spirituality highly relevant today. Although Ignatius of Loyola, the founder of the Jesuits, is generally credited with popularizing discernment, discernment was practiced in Benedictine monasteries for many, many years before him.

The Rule, the Abbot, and the Novitiate: Benedictine Community Life

Benedict believed that his Rule would help monks in community become free, as they would not have to wonder how to handle various situations which arose. The Rule would have already taken such situations into account and provided the monks with the guidance they needed. Thus, the Benedictine Rule is lengthy, comprehensive, highly structured, and rigorous. Living in community is rigorous—it is neither an easy nor a physically comfortable way of life. For example, the monks were to live in joy, but laughter was not permitted, because Benedict believed that the spiritual life was serious business. Tears of sorrow for one's sinfulness were seen as a gift from God, a notion that might seem strange to us today.

The head of the monastery was the abbot. He was elected to the position on the basis of his holiness and fidelity to the gospel. For that reason, he was seen as another Christ, a person to whom the men in community owed obedience. Benedict firmly believed that God's wishes for the community came through the abbot, and that those in community should humbly recognize this authority. Although important decisions involved the entire community, a final decision was always made by the abbot. The overarching goal was to live together in love and in the presence of God.

Because Benedict saw the glory of God in everyday life, the community both worked and prayed together. A typical day in his monastery consisted of four hours of liturgical prayer, four hours of spiritual reading, and six hours of work. Work consisted of whatever needed to be done in order to keep the monastery functioning well. Meals were to be eaten in community, but taken in silence so that each person could better hear God speaking to him.

A man wishing to join Benedict's community needed to go through a twelve-month period of discernment and testing. This was known as a *novitiate*. Prospective community members were called *novices;* they were supervised by a novice master. Questions that the seeker would be asked included: "Why are you here?" "Do you seek God? How so?" "Are you eager to do the work of God?" "Are you ready, even eager, to obey freely rather than seek your own interest?" "Are you ready for trials which will destroy your self-importance or pride?" (Costello 70). As we can see, these are questions we can ask ourselves today, even though most of us do not live in monasteries.

The Liturgy of the Hours: Communal Prayer

Organizing the prayer traditions of the Desert Fathers (Christian ascetics who lived and prayed in the Egyptian and Syrian deserts), Benedict organized the Liturgy of the Hours, also known as the Divine Office, or the "Work of God." The Liturgy of the Hours was (and still is) the common prayer of the Benedictine community. The liturgy is a set of prescribed prayers (drawn especially from the Psalms and certain gospel readings) and hymns used at certain set times during the day. Between the psalms and the scripture readings, some complicated chants were sung. Originally, Benedict devised eight "hours" of prayer. Their original names are as follows:

> *Matins* (prayed during the night)
> *Lauds* (prayed at dawn)

Prime (early morning prayer)
Terce (mid-morning prayer)
Sext (mid-day prayer)
None (mid-afternoon prayer)
Vespers (evening prayer)
C*ompline* (night prayer before retiring)

The members of Benedict's communities certainly prayed often, even to the point of having their sleep interrupted! But that was part of the commitment of placing God above all things, even one's self-comfort.

The Second Vatican Council of 1962–1965 eliminated the hour of *prime*, thereby reducing the number of hours to seven, of which three are major hours (*matins, lauds,* and *vespers)* while the remaining are minor hours. The Council declared that *vespers* and *lauds* are the most fundamental parts of all the "hours." Today, the Divine Office is a prayer that all Catholics are encouraged to pray, not just the ordained or vowed religious. There are books with the prayers and scripture readings for each hour of each day which can be obtained at any Catholic bookstore. The modern structure of an "hour" is usually a hymn, two psalms, and a canticle (Old Testament in the morning; New Testament in the evening), followed by intercessions, a prayer, and a blessing (McBrien 790).

Lectio Divina

The method of personal prayer that uses the discipline of spiritual reading as its foundation is called *lectio divina,* or "holy reading."

Lectio divina is not simply spiritual reading. Rather, it is a structured way to meet God in scripture. Classic lectio divina had five steps, while the more modern version adds a final, sixth step. The steps of lectio divina are:

Silence: Silencing one's body as well as one's mind is key. We must be both interiorly and exteriorly silent if we are to hear God speaking through what we are reading. In many ways, getting rid of external noise is easier to accomplish than getting rid of all the anxieties in our minds. Yet, both must be minimized if we are to hear God. Our world and our minds are loud, busy places. It will take a while to learn to quiet them.

Reading: We then read a scriptural passage; it may be just a few words in length. We are not to read for speed or to cover much material. Rather we are to read slowly, savoring each word, reading the passage *as the passage reads us*. Does that sound strange? It isn't strange at all if we can recall a time when we read a passage that seemed to have been written expressly for us, a passage that spoke to us in just the way we needed. Much of scripture can be experienced this way, but this is much more likely to occur if we take the time to slow down.

Meditation: After reading the passage, we reflect on it, perhaps even imagining ourselves as a character in it. In other words, we try to imagine what was going on so as to precipitate the event described in the passage or to evoke the passage's meaning.

Prayer: We then pray over the passage, asking God to reveal to us whatever message God would have us take from it. This is a brief prayer, something like, "Help me to be open to what you would have me learn."

Contemplation: We then quiet ourselves and permit God to speak to us. The goal is to empty ourselves of our own preconceived notions of what we are to take from the passage, and instead open ourselves to God's word of love to us.

Incarnation: In this later-added step, we live out what we have learned by doing concrete acts of service in the world.

Lectio divina is a spiritual practice in which any of us can engage. Although it requires time and discipline, its benefits far outweigh the sacrifices we might have to make to dedicate ourselves to it.

As an example of lectio divina, let's say that the passage we are encountering is the post-resurrection story of Jesus' encounter with Peter from the Gospel of John (Jn 21:15–18). In that passage, Jesus asks Peter three times if Peter loves him. Peter responds in the affirmative each time, but prior to responding the third time, scripture tells us that Peter was "hurt" that Jesus had asked him the question three times. As we use this passage for lectio, we would first enter into external and internal silence. Then, we would read the passage carefully and slowly, letting it "read" us. In other words, we would look for what "jumps out" at us from this story. After that, we might meditate on the encounter between Jesus and Peter. How would we have felt if we had been Peter, who had denied Jesus three times (after swearing he would not do so just a few hours prior to his denial), and now was being asked repeatedly whether he loved Jesus? Have we denied Jesus? How would we feel if Jesus asked us repeatedly whether we loved him? Following this, we might pray briefly, asking God to permit us to receive from this gift of scripture what God would have us receive. Then, we become quiet, giving God the space and time to speak to us. We might end the lectio with the Lord's Prayer, and then commit ourselves to demonstrating our love for Christ in a tangible way.

The Importance of Humility at All Times

Benedict taught community members about the "ladder of humility," a twelve-rung ladder that would help an individual to "reach" humility, just as a ladder helps us to reach objects out of our grasp. The rungs of the ladder describe how a person should behave toward God and others. Benedict chose this image to be reminiscent of Jacob's ladder in the Hebrew scripture, a ladder that led to heaven upon which God's messengers were moving up and down (Gen 28:12). Here are Benedict's own words about the ladder of humility, contained in chapter seven of *The Rule of St. Benedict*:

> (1) The first degree of humility, then, is that a man have the fear of God before his eyes, shunning all forgetfulness and that he be ever mindful of all that God has commanded. . . . (2) the second degree of humility is when a man love not his own will nor is pleased to fulfill his own desires. . . . (3) the third degree of humility is that for the love of God a man subjects himself to a superior in all obedience, imitating the Lord of whom the apostle says, 'He became obedient even unto death.' . . . (4) the fourth degree of humility is, that, if hard and distasteful things are commanded, nay, even thought injuries are inflicted, he shall accept them with patience and even temper, and not grow weary or give up. . . .

> (5) The fifth degree of humility is, when one hides from his abbot none of the evil thoughts which arise in his heart or the evils committed by him in secret, but humbly confesses them. . . . (6) the sixth degree of humility is, when a monk is content with the meanest and worst of everything. . . . (7) the seventh degree of humility is, when, not only his tongue he declares, but also in his inmost soul believes, that he is the lowest and vilest of men, humbling himself. . . . (8) the eighth degree of humility is, when a monk does nothing but what is sanctioned by the common rule of the monastery and the example of his elders.

> (9) The ninth degree of humility is, when a monk withholds his tongue from speaking, and keeping silence does not speak until he is asked.

. . . (10) the tenth degree of humility is, when a monk is not easily moved or quick for laughter. . . . (11) the eleventh degree of humility is, that, when a monks speaks, he speaks gently and without laughter, humbly and with gravity, and with few and sensible words, and that he not be loud. . . . (12) the twelfth degree of humility is, when a monk is not only humble of heart but always let it appear also in his whole exterior to all that see him; namely, at the Work of God [i.e., Divine Office], in the garden, on a journey, in the field, or wherever he may be, sitting, walking, or standing, let him always have his head bowed down, his eyes focused on the ground, ever holding himself guilty of his sins. . . .

Having, therefore, ascended all these degrees of humility, the monk will presently arrive at that love of God, which being perfect, casts out fear (1 Jn 4:18). In virtue of this love all things which at first he observed not without fear, he will now begin to keep without any effort, and as it were, naturally by force of habit, no longer from the fear of hell, but from the love of Christ, from the very habit of good and the pleasure in virtue (Verheyen 221).

Seen in these ways, the Benedictine monastery is really a school in which people learn how to serve God and one another with awe, joy, and love. It is also a place in which people learn to regard everything in creation with reverence and awe, and treat it accordingly. Because God is good, and God willed all that exists to be, we are to show reverence to all that God has brought into being.

Well-Known Benedictines

Anselm of Canterbury (1033–1109): A brilliant Benedictine theologian, who was also the archbishop of Canterbury, and one of the Doctors of the Church. Regarded by some historians as one of

the earliest Scholastics of the Middle Ages, he is a theologian identified with a particular theological and philosophical movement.

Bede Griffiths (1906–1993): A Benedictine monk and priest
who was a co-founder of a Christian ashram in India and a pioneer
in the inter-faith dialogue between Christianity and Eastern faith
traditions.

References for Learning More about Benedictine Spirituality

Kardong, Terrence. "Benedictine Spirituality" in Michael Downey,
ed. *The New Dictionary of Catholic Spirituality*. Collegeville,
MN: Liturgical Press, 1993.

Nugent, Andrew. "Benedictine Spirituality" in Stephen Costello,
ed. *The Search for Spirituality: Seven Paths within the Catholic
Tradition*. Dublin: Liffey Press, 2002. 57–82.

The Rule of St. Benedict, 1949 ed. Rev. Boniface Verheyen, OSB,
trans. Accessed at www.kansasmonks.org/?page_id=221

Stewart, Columba. *Prayer and Community: The Benedictine Community*. Maryknoll, NY: Orbis Books, 1998.

Swan, Laura, and Phyllis Zagano. *The Benedictine Tradition* (Spirituality in History Series). Collegeville, MN: Liturgical Press,
2007.

Vanderwilt, Jeffrey T. "Liturgy of the Hours" in Richard P. McBrien.
The HarperCollins Encyclopedia of Catholicism. New York:
HarperCollins, 1995.

three

Cistercian Spirituality

The Cistercians and Their World

Unlike Augustinian and Benedictine spiritualities, Cistercian spirituality is named for a place rather than a person. Cistercian spirituality represents a reform of Benedictine spirituality initiated largely by Saint Bernard of Clairvaux (1090–1153).

Over time, observance of the Rule established by Benedict of Nursia had become lax. The monastery at Monte Cassino had been destroyed by invading barbarian tribes, the result being that each monastery developed its own rule and traditions. When Charlemagne came into power, a former member of his court, Benedict of Aniane (750–821), tried—without success—to return to the rigor of the original Benedictine Rule in a monastery he founded. Once Charlemagne backed his efforts, Benedict insisted that monasteries follow a common Rule (the Benedictine) and that there should be one abbot (himself) over all others.

After Benedict's death, these reforms also fell into laxity, especially because of the interference of political figures and the wealthy nobility in monastic affairs. Attempts at reform were evident, especially at the monastery at Cluny, which became the central monastery of the Benedictine Order, an order that included many smaller monasteries. But even Cluny eventually experienced difficulties in adhering to the strict Benedictine Rule. This distressed Bernard of Clairvaux, who felt that there should be a return to the spirit and rigor of the original Benedictine rule to recover the purity of the order. Bernard eventually led a group of men who shared his zeal for the original Benedictine Rule, and they settled in Citeaux, from which this spirituality receives its name.

Bernard combined a contemplative spirit with a pastoral heart. He used the image of a canal to make his point about the active life: "Why, if you are wise, will you be a reservoir and not a canal? Because at one and the same time, the canal pours out what it receives, but the reservoir retains the water till it is full and then communicates the overflow without damage to itself or disadvantage" (DeWaal 86).

Bernard believed that human beings were made in the image and likeness of God and that our desire for God comes from God. He emphasized this in the following passage.

> The first point to consider is this, that God deserves exceeding love from us, a love that has no measure. . . . He was first to love. He, who is so great, loves us so much. . . . He, the unmeasured and eternal God, he who is love beyond all human ken, whose greatness knows no bounds, whose wisdom has no end, loves. Shall we, then, set a limit on our love for him? . . . I will love thee with all the power thou hast given me; not worthily, for that can never be, but to the full of my capacity. . . . I will love thee more and more, as thou seest fit to give the further power; yet never, never, as thou shouldst be loved."
> (DeWaal 110–111)

He was Augustinian in his confidence in God's grace and in his devotion to Christ.

> [Christ] was incomprehensible and inaccessible, invisible and completely unthinkable. Now he wishes to be comprehended, wishes to be seen, wishes to be thought about. How, do you ask? As lying in the manger, resting in the Virgin's lap, preaching

on the mountain, praying through the night, or
hanging on the cross, growing pale in death, free
among the dead and ruling in hell, and also rising
on the third day, showing the apostles the place of
his nails, the signs of victory, and finally as ascend-
ing over heaven's secrets in their sight. (DeWaal
96–97)

Bernard wrote many sermons on the book of the Song of Songs,
which, he believed, revealed the love between God and humanity
and, indeed, each person.

To encourage a single focus on God, Bernard emphasized separation from the world and solitude. For Bernard, asceticism was
necessary, for he believed that every monk's life should have a lent-
en quality (Kinsella 128). Cistercian monks took vows of conversion to Christ, obedience to superiors, and stability (i.e., spending
one's entire life in the same monastery). Monastic reform also included poverty, membership of lay brothers, simplified liturgies that
followed the liturgical seasons, time for study (but only as it served
God), a polity of community (all members agreed to a reform), and
visitation of all monasteries by the abbot of the founding monastery.
The lay brothers lived a community life and did much work in the
monastery, as they witnessed their fidelity to Christ through their
service of manual labor.

Service to others was paramount. "But for our love of others to
be wholly right, God must be at its root. No one can love his neighbor perfectly, unless it is in God he holds him dear. And nobody can
love his fellow-man in God, who loves not God himself. We must
begin by loving God; and then, we shall be able, in him, to love our
neighbor too" (DeWaal 115).

In terms of poverty, the only income for the monastery came
from the monks' labor; no external sources for income were permitted. The monks ate simple foods, wore simple clothing, and lived
in modest buildings. Their libraries, however, were well stocked,
as the monks hand-copied the Bible, liturgical books, and patristic
works. As mentioned previously, lay brothers were accepted to help

with the monks' labor, especially in the areas of farming and fishing. These lay brothers followed the same rules as did the monks, except they had less involvement in liturgies due to their lack of education.

In terms of simplified liturgies, Cistercian monks engaged in simple chant, one that was simpler than the prevalent Gregorian chant. The liturgies themselves were designed to help a monk make the connection between the liturgical season and his own life. Daily Mass and communal participation in the Divine Office were emphasized.

In the seventeenth century, further Cistercian reform was made by monks in the abbey La Grande Trappe in France. This was the beginning of the Trappist order, highlighted by austerity, silence, and contemplation. Eventually, the Cistercians split into two groups: the Order of Citeaux (O.Cist.), whose members were active in education and priestly work; and the Order of Strict Observance (O.C.S.O.), the Trappists.

Hallmarks of Cistercian Spirituality

Cistercian spirituality desires God above all, recognizing that God has desired us first.

If God, who is so great and has no need of us, loves and desires us, we should do everything in our power to respond to God with love. To do this, we must learn to desire God above everything else.

Cistercian spirituality is devoted to Mary.

Christ is the model of what it means to be a person of integrity, one whose words and actions match each other. His mother is also an example of humility and obedience—attributes that are important in the Cistercian tradition. In particular, the humble Mary of modest means obeyed God perfectly, even when she did not know what the eventual outcome would be.

Cistercian spirituality values a lifelong relationship with scripture.

Those adhering to the Cistercian way are not only to read and pray scripture; they are to have a relationship with it. We have a relationship with anyone or anything in which there can be mutuality. Praying scripture using lectio divina permits such a relationship, since, in doing so, scripture can speak to the one doing the lectio.

Cistercian spirituality highlights the importance of prayer, especially contemplation.

All communities founded on *The Rule of St. Benedict* understand the importance of prayer. One type of prayer, *contemplation*, is considered to be a gift from God, in that it is considered to be a direct experience with God that God alone brings about. As such, human beings cannot "make it happen" by using human-made formulas or metaphors. It cannot be achieved by saying holy words or thinking holy thoughts, even though these might be very good in helping us grow spiritually. Many spiritual masters see contemplation as something that cannot, in the end, be *achieved* at all—at least not in the conventional sense of the word.

Nevertheless, prayer forms have been suggested over the centuries to help individuals be prepared, should God wish to give the gift of contemplation. The important prayer forms associated with the Benedictine tradition have been described earlier: the Liturgy of the Hours (Divine Office) and lectio divina. Modern Cistercian contemplative practices have been developed by the Trappist Basil Pennington, who has written much on "centering prayer" (see below), as well as by the Trappist Thomas Merton.

Cistercian spirituality cultivates radical simplicity.

Cistercians embrace simplicity in living conditions, dress, food, and work. Because spiritual growth must first be preceded by the ability to encounter God in daily living, all external distractions must be minimized. That is why both exterior and interior silence is so highly valued, for only in this way can spiritual growth flourish. One must learn that what is important is what is interior, not exterior.

Cistercian spirituality highlights the importance of pastoral activities, especially hospitality.

Because God was first hospitable to us, we should be hospitable to others. In the monasteries, even though monks were secluded from the world, they always saw hospitality to those who came to their doors as their joyful duty. That can be true for us today as well.

Cistercian Spirituality emphasizes the integration of the active and contemplative.

Cistercians do not have their "heads in the clouds." They work (hard) and are practical in their approach to life. Yet, they understand that all depends on God and are willing to surrender themselves to God in whatever way God sees fit. This type of integration is one that any of us—Cistercian or not—could adopt.

In her book *The Way of Simplicity*, Esther DeWaal quotes the twelfth-century Cistercian Aelred of Rievaulx on this point:

> All our good works consist in two things, namely in the active and the contemplative life. The active life is like wool clothing; the contemplative life is like linen clothing; the former is rougher, the latter more comfortable; the former exterior, the latter interior. The active life can indeed suffice against the coldness of damnation and can wipe away all the shamefulness of sins; without the active life, the contemplative life cannot, in this mortal domain, lead anyone to perfection. (84)

Well-Known Cistercians/Trappists

Aelred of Rievaulx (1110–1167): Cistercian monk who wrote much about the integrated life and about spiritual friendship. In thinking about the integrated life, using the gospel story of Mary and Martha, Aelred wrote:

> You see if Mary had been alone in the house, no one would have fed the Lord; if Martha had been alone,

no one would have tasted his presence and his words. Martha thus represents the action, the labor accomplished for Christ, Mary the repose that frees from bodily labor, in order to taste the sweetness of the Lord in reading, prayer, and contemplation. That is why, my brothers, so long as Christ is on earth, poor, subject to hunger, to thirst, to temptation, it is necessary that these two women inhabit the same house, that in one soul the two activities occur. . . .

Do not neglect Mary for Martha, nor Martha for Mary. If you neglect Martha, who will serve Jesus? And if you neglect Mary, what will be the use of the visit of Jesus, since you will not taste his sweetness? Know, my brothers, that in this life, it is necessary never to separate these two women. (De-Waal 80–81)

It must be remembered that Martha labored and Mary was free from work in the same house; in the same soul in which Christ is welcomed, both lives are led, each in its own time, place, and order. (De-Waal 85)

About spiritual friendship, Aelred wrote:

The perfecting and extending of true friendship is the great and wondrous happiness that we look for in the life to come. God himself is at work, pouring out himself and the creature he has raised up between the various hierarchies of his creation, and between each and every one of his elect such reciprocal friendship and charity that each loves the other as himself. Each, in consequence, rejoices in his neighbor's happiness as his own, so that the bliss of each is shared by all, and the sum total of that bliss is everyone's. This is the true and everlasting friendship, which has its beginnings here, and its consummation hereafter. And if such reciprocity is hard to come by in this world (since it is laid up for us beyond!), should not our happiness grow accordingly? (DeWaal 123–24)

That a person may love himself, the love of God is formed in him; that one may love one's neighbor, the capacity of one's heart is enlarged. Then as this divine fire grows warmer little by little, it wondrously absorbs the other loves into its fullness, like so many sparks. And so it leads all the soul's love with it to that supreme and ineffable good, where neither self nor neighbor is loved for self or for neighbor, but only insofar as each fades away from self and is totally borne into God. Meanwhile, these three loves are engendered by one another, nourished by one another; and fanned into flame by one another. Then they are all brought to perfection together. (DeWaal 147)

May my thoughts and my speech, leisure and labor, my acts and reflections, my prosperity and my adversity, my life and my death, my health and my sickness, and whatsoever else is mine; that I exist, that I live, that I feel, that I understand; let all be devoted to them and all be spent for them, for whom thou thyself did not disdain to spend thyself. (DeWaal 148)

Thomas Merton (1915–1968): Modern Trappist monk, who because of his many writings appealed to non-monastics, even to this day. We will read more from Merton in the chapter on mysticism, but here is an excerpt from his book *No Man Is an Island*. It might come as a surprise that a monk who embraced solitude wrote so passionately about the need for others.

When Jesus said, "He that would save his life will lose it, and he that would lose his life for my sake shall find it" . . . God's will for us is not only that we should be the persons He means us to be, but that we should share in His work of creation and *help*

Him to make us into the persons He means us to be. Always, and in all things, God's will for me is that I should shape my own destiny, work out my own salvation, forge my own eternal happiness, in the way He has planned it for me. And since no man is an island, since we all depend on one another, I cannot work out God's will in my own life unless I also consciously help other men to work out His will in theirs. His will, then, is our sanctification, our transformation in Christ, our deeper and fuller integration with other men. And this integration results not in the absorption and disappearance of our own personality, but in its affirmation and its perfection. Everything that God wills in my life is directed to this double end: my perfection as part of a universal whole, and my perfection in myself as an individual person, made in God's image and likeness. (64)

Basil Pennington (1931–2005): Trappist monk who wrote much about centering prayer, firmly believing that it belongs to all of God's people, not just those in monasteries. Here are several descriptions of centering prayer (taken from *Call to the Center*) in Pennington's words: "Centering prayer is a very pure prayer—pure gift, the total gift of self to God" (34). "Centering prayer is listening to a call—the call letting everything else go, simply listening, 'Be still and know that I am God'" (15).

Our most private room is that deep place within us, what we have been calling our center. 'There, indeed, our Father dwells.' And we are invited to go to that center, shut out all else, and abide there with our Father in prayer. With the use of our prayer word, we, as it were, close the door, or to use another image, we create a cloud of unknowing, leaving everything outside ourselves, quietly and peacefully within with the Father. (56–57)

Pennington developed rules for centering prayer. In them, we find traces of his Trappist background.

> Sit relaxed and be quiet,
>
> 1. Be in faith and love to God who dwells in the center of your being.
> 2. Take up a love word and let it be gently present, supporting your being to God in faith-filled love.
> 3. Whenever you become *aware* of anything, simply, gently return to the Lord with your prayer word.
>
> Let the Our Father (or some other prayer) pray itself. (*Centered Living* 54)

References for Learning More about Cistercian/ Trappist Spirituality

Casey, Michael. "Cisterician Spirituality" in Michael Downey, ed. *The New Dictionary of Catholic Spirituality.* Collegeville, MN: Liturgical Press, 1993.

DeWaal, Esther. *The Way of Simplicity: The Cistercian Tradition.* Maryknoll, NY: Orbis Books, 1998.

Kinsella, Nivard. "Cistercian Spirituality" in Stephen Costello, ed. *The Search for Spirituality: Seven Paths within the Catholic Tradition.* Dublin, Ireland: Liffey Press, 2002. 115–134.

Merton, Thomas. *No Man Is an Island.* New York: Harcourt, Inc., 1983.

Pennington, M. Basil. *Call to the Center.* New York: Doubleday, 1990.

_____. *Centered Living: The Way of Centering Prayer.* Liguori, MO: Liguori Publications, 1999.

four

Carmelite Spirituality

Carmel: The Founders and Their World

Around the year 1200, a group of lay hermits gathered at Mt. Carmel in Haifa—a city that still exists today as part of modern-day Israel. They had gathered to follow a formula for communal life given by Albert, Patriarch of Jerusalem. This formula for living included obedience, silence, solitude, prayer (especially praying the psalms), fasting, poverty, sharing of material goods, manual labor, asceticism, fraternal love, service to the poor (in imitation of Christ), and devotion to Christ (especially demonstrated by daily eucharist) (Egan 228). Because of the association of the Old Testament prophet Elijah with Mt Carmel, he was considered to be the group's model and "founder." Devotion to Mary (as the model of devotion to Christ) was also part of the charism, and was signified by the dedication of the chapel at Mt. Carmel to her.

Political unrest forced the group to leave the Holy Land and migrate to Europe and England in the 1300s. Concomitant with the move, the formula given by Albert became a rule, and the group became an order. Carmelites were permitted to live in towns in communal dwellings, where they could eat and pray together. These early Carmelites could travel for pastoral ministry and worked as teachers, preachers, and sacramental ministers. Because of the need to travel, monastic practices had to be modified, although the insistence on individual and communal poverty was not changed. The Carmelites

41

saw the need to embrace both silence and solitude in the midst of their preaching and teaching. Like other orders, over time, the Carmelites became lax in their practices. Reform was needed, and in the 1500s, two persons of towering ability appeared to provide it.

Teresa of Avila

By the late fifteenth century, women had been accepted into the Carmelite order. Teresa of Avila (1515–1582) was a Carmelite whose own conversion was prompted, in part, by a serious illness. According to her own *Autobiography,* Teresa had entered the convent as a boarding student in 1531. Although she was inspired by a particular nun, she was not convinced that she was called to the same life. "All the nuns were pleased with me; for the Lord had given me grace, wherever I was, to please people, and so I became a great favorite. Although at the time, I had the greatest possible aversion from being a nun" (72). After eighteen months there, Theresa became ill and while recuperating, she decided to enter the convent. "This decision, then, to renter the religious life seems to have been inspired more by servile fear [of damnation] than of love" (75).

Eventually, in 1536, she entered a Carmelite convent, but soon after, although she described her happiness in the convent, she suffered many physical, emotional, and spiritual ailments. Many treatments were tried, and most failed to bring her any relief. During her illness, especially after she returned to her convent, Teresa did much spiritual reading (particularly Augustine's *Confessions*) and reflection, especially meditating on the suffering Christ and God's loving presence.

Her *Autobiography* makes clear that, at this time, Teresa was vain, wanting others to think well of her. She realized that her heart was torn in terms of her devotion to God and her devotion to the ways of the world. Her prayer life had become perfunctory. Even within her Carmelite community, Teresa noted that there were many distractions to tempt her, especially visitors to the convent and the social cliques of the outside world that operated within the convent as well. It took a number of years—and God's grace—to help her overcome these obstacles.

Over the course of these years, Teresa spoke with a number of spiritual directors about the desire to grow in intimacy with God, but some of these directors completely failed to understand her. When Teresa began having more intense spiritual experiences, she could not speak freely about them as doing so placed her at risk. At the time, inward spiritual experiences and individual reading of scripture were held suspect as being too "Protestant" by the Inquisition.

She eventually received permission to found a new community based on the original Carmelite rule proposed by Albert and immediately set out to do so. Teresa's new community was characterized by devotion to Christ, prayer, earthiness, healthy human relationships, joy, and warmth; she was highly suspicious of any "holier-than-thou" or gloomy attitudes! Teresa understood that her little community was connected to the larger body of Christ; for that reason, cultivating love among the various members in her community was absolutely necessary.

For Teresa, the more one is aware of the indwelling of God, the more one is eager to serve God and others because one sees God in others. Furthermore, friendship with God permits one to share in the life of the Trinity, which means seeing God in everyone. This was a theme emphasized by Augustine as well. Teresa wrote much about these themes for her Carmelite community. These works include her *Autobiography*, *The Way of Perfection*, as well as *The Interior Castle*. In *Castle*, Teresa describes movement to God by use of an analogy with seven rooms of a castle, with the outermost rooms precluding the spiritual life and the four innermost rooms signifying increasing union with God. Although profound, her writings also contain elements of humor. Teresa emphasized the Prayer of the Quiet, which is profound contemplation. She described it in chapter 31 of *The Way of Perfection*:

> Now, daughters, I still want to describe this Prayer
> of the Quiet . . . as the Lord has been pleased to
> teach it to me, perhaps in order that I might describe

it to you. It is in this kind of prayer, as I said, that the Lord seems to begin to show us that He is hearing our petition. . . . This is a supernatural state, and however hard we try, we cannot reach it for ourselves, for it is a state in which the soul enters into peace, or rather in which the Lord gives it peace through His presence. . . . In this state, all the faculties are stilled. The soul, in a way which has nothing to do with the outward senses, realizes that it is now very close to its God, and that, if it were but a little closer, it would become one with Him through union. . . .

It is, as it were, in a swoon, both inwardly and outwardly. . . . The body experiences the greatest delight and the soul is conscious of a deep satisfaction. . . . There seems nothing left for it to desire. The faculties are stilled and have no wish to move, for any movement they may make appears to hinder the soul from loving God. . . .

Persons in this state prefer the body to remain motionless, for otherwise their peace would be destroyed: for this reason, they dare not stir. Speaking is a distress to them: they will spend a whole hour on a single repetition of the Paternoster. . . . Sometimes tears come to their eyes, but they weep very gently and quite without distress: their whole desire is the hallowing of this name. They seem not to be in the world, and have no wish to hear or see anything but their God; nothing distresses them, nor does it seem that anything can possibly do so.

Teresa believed that the more one befriended God, the more that God would grant this gift of the Prayer of the Quiet.

John of the Cross

John of the Cross (1542–1591) is considered to be the co-founder of the reformed Carmelite community begun by Teresa of Avila. He is also one of Christianity's greatest mystical theologians. His poem *Dark Night of the Soul* has inspired spiritual seekers throughout the centuries.

John founded a monastery based on the original Carmelite ideal as proposed by Albert, and attempted to correct the laxity that had crept into observance of the Carmelite rule by communities of men. Because of his enormous zeal for God, John was imprisoned by those in his own community who disagreed with his reforms. He later escaped and was hidden by nuns until it was safe for him to re-emerge. Yet, it was precisely his experience of rejection that paved the way for his spirituality with its mystical elements and its poetry. In fact, John is considered Spain's greatest poet. His writings include *Spiritual Canticle, Ascent of Mt. Carmel*, and *Dark Night of the Soul*.

This is the beginning of *Dark Night of the Soul*:

> On a dark night, kindled in love with yearnings —
>   oh, happy chance!
> I went forth without being observed, my house be-
>   ing now at rest.
> In darkness and secure, by the secret ladder, dis-
>   guised — oh, happy chance!
> In darkness and in concealment, my house being
>   now at rest.
> In the happy night, in secret when none saw me
> Nor I beheld aught, without light or guide, save
>   that which burned in my heart.
> This light guided me more surely than the light of
>   noonday
> To a place where he (well I knew who!) was await-
>   ing me.
> A place where none appeared.

Oh, night that guided me, oh, night more lovely
than the dawn,
Oh, night that joined Beloved with lover, lover
transformed in the Beloved!
Upon my flowery breast, kept wholly for himself
alone,
There he stayed sleeping, and I caressed him. And
the fanning of the cedars made a breeze.
The breeze blew from the turret, as I parted his
locks;
With his gentle hand, he wounded my neck and
caused all my senses to be suspended.
I remained, lost in oblivion; my face reclined on
the Beloved.
All ceased, and I abandoned myself, leaving my
cares forgotten among the lilies.

The last two stanzas present ideas that are reminiscent of Teresa: "suspended senses/faculties" and "all ceased and I abandoned myself" seem not to be of this world. Clearly, they are saying something about the same phenomenon: an encounter with God that mere words and normal human experiences cannot describe.

For John, the dark night of the soul is God's initiative of our liberation from worldly attachments so that we can be totally God-centered. Although God uses the Church, scripture, and the sacraments to reach each person, God also gives each person grace uniquely particular to him or her in whatever life situation that the person finds him- or herself. We cannot achieve a state of union with God intellectually or by our own efforts. We can only love God in a spiritually mature way when we are free of external attachments to the world and attachments to ourselves.

In this dark night, everything might seem to fall apart (as it did for John). It may seem as if God is absent. We seek God, but cannot find any comfort. The God who once seemed so present in our lives seems entirely absent. John felt that this was to purify us so that we will be satisfied with God alone. The dark night is associated with affliction, confusion, and frustration, as our comfort zones are stripped away. The passive night of the senses is a time when our busyness moves toward contemplation, while the passive night of the spirit is a time when we are purified. We lose possessiveness and gain freedom and maturity. This sounds unpleasant, but the closer one draws to God, the more one can enjoy life in this "night."

John believed that there were three spiritual stages: the purgative way, when we realize the wrongs we have done and express sorrow; the illuminative way, when God continues to reveal more about himself to us; and the unitive way, when we move toward union with God. In the end, how we love one another and how we love God are reciprocal, and we need an experience of human tenderness to move us toward God. The closer we come to God, the more compassionate we become to others.

Hallmarks of Carmelite Spirituality

Carmelite spirituality is devoted to Christ.

For a Christian, Christ is the beginning and the end of the spiritual life. His love for us was demonstrated through his incarnation and his passion and death on the cross. His desire to become one with us and his continued desire for intimacy with us should evoke a profound desire on our part for greater intimacy with him. He chose us; he loved us *first*.

Carmelite spirituality is devoted to Mary.

In Mary's assent to God, she is a model of perfect obedience. In her giving birth to Jesus, she is the first disciple, bringing Christ to the world. In her faithfulness to her Son at the cross, she is a model of living in the hope of things to come. These are all important attributes for Carmelites.

Carmelite spirituality seeks God above all things.

Everything that exists does so because God wills it to be. Although all things are not God (pantheism), all things reflect something of God in their being. If we open our eyes (and hearts), we begin to encounter God in everything, even in the ordinary things and tasks of life. If we pay attention to the people and creatures around us, we encounter the God who loved them into existence.

Carmelite spirituality is aware of the indwelling God.

"The Kingdom of God is within," Jesus said. We need to come to terms with the reality that God is both transcendent (totally other) and immanent (within us). In other words, God is beyond anything that we can fathom, but God is as intimate as our next breath. As we gain greater appreciation for God's indwelling, we respect others and love them more perfectly. After all, if God lives in us, then God lives in others. If God has chosen to love others into existence and to make his dwelling in them, who are we to treat them shabbily?

Carmelite spirituality values compassionate listening to others through loving service.

Just as God listens to us, so, too, are we to listen to others compassionately, to suffer with them, serving them in whatever way we can. In all this, we are to be humble in our encounters with others, being with them without trying to "fix" them or without having the (erroneous) impression that we know best what others should do. In every encounter with others, we recognize that God is also present and act accordingly. In this way, we live Matthew 25: "Whatever you did to the least of these, you did to me."

Carmelite spirituality encourages listening to God through silence, solitude, and contemplation.

Because God is gracious and listens to us, we must resist the temptation to be the ones constantly speaking, telling God what we know, what we need, what others should do, and what God should do! In humility, we must be silent, still, and patient and let God be God. We also need to ask for God's help in overcoming anything that prevents us from achieving stillness.

Carmelite spirituality commands: Love always!

God loves us first, and that is why we are here. Christ loves us and died for us, securing our redemption. The Spirit loves us, accompanying and guiding us every step along the way. Showered with so much love, we are to love God and others without holding back. Even — and especially — when others are difficult or choose to act in evil ways, we are to love. After all, God loves us when we sin against him, especially when we are difficult or treat others badly.

Other Well-Known Carmelites

Thérèse of Lisieux (1873–1897): A Carmelite nun who was also known as the "Little Flower." Because she could not do great things (in the world's estimation) for God, she resolved to do little things with great love. True to her Carmelite tradition, she is both mystical and full of love, as evidenced in the words from her own autobiography:

> "But I will look for some means of going to heaven by a little way which is very short and very straight. . . ." (114) "I am a very little soul who can only offer very little things to God." (143) "I have found my vocation. My vocation is love! . . . I will be love." (155)
>
> Love proves itself by deeds, so how am I to show my love? Well, I will scatter flowers, perfuming the divine throne with their fragrance, and I'll sweetly sing my hymn of love. Yes, my Beloved, that is how I'll spend my short life. The only way I can prove my love is by scattering flowers, and these flowers are every little sacrifice, every glance and word, and the doing of the least of actions for love. I wish both to suffer and to find joy through love. Thus will I scatter my flowers. (156)

Edith Stein (1891–1942): A Carmelite nun (Sister Teresa Benedicta of the Cross) who was a Jewish convert to Catholicism. An excellent teacher and writer, she wrote extensively on philosophical and theological matters. She was arrested by the Nazis (because she was Jewish) and executed at Auschwitz.

References for Learning More about Carmelite Spirituality

Egan, Keith. "Carmelite Spirituality" in Michael Downey, ed. *The New Dictionary of Catholic Spirituality*. Collegeville, MN: Liturgical Press, 1993.

____. "Carmelite Order" in Richard P. McBrien, ed. *The Harper-Collins Encyclopedia of Catholicism*. New York: HarperCollins, 1995.

John of the Cross. *Dark Night of the Soul: A Masterpiece in the Literature of Mysticism by St. John of the Cross*. E. Allison Peers, trans. New York: Image Books, 1959.

McGreal, Wilfrid. *At the Fountain of Elijah: The Carmelite Tradition*. Maryknoll, NY: Orbis Books, 1999.

McGreal, Wilfrid. "Carmelite Spirituality" in Stephen Costello, ed. *The Search for Spirituality: Seven Paths within the Catholic Tradition*. Dublin, Ireland: Liffey Press, 2002. 83–113.

Teresa of Avila. *The Life of Teresa of Jesus*. New York: Image Books, 1991.

____. *Way of Perfection*. New York: Image Books, 1991.

Thérèse of Lisieux. *The Autobiography of Saint Thérèse of Lisieux: The Story of a Soul*. John Beevers, trans. New York: Image Books, 1987.

five

Dominican Spirituality

Dominic and His World

Dominic de Guzman (1170–1221) was a highly spiritual child, and all who knew him felt that he was destined for a career in the Church. As soon as he was old enough, Dominic was educated by an uncle who was a priest. After his ordination, Dominic accompanied his bishop on a diplomatic mission in the early 1200s. When the pair encountered a group of Christian heretics, they decided to win them over to orthodoxy through their witness of voluntary poverty and effective preaching. Over the course of the next ten years, this work led Dominic to found an order of preachers who would move from place to place, unusual at the time, since only bishops were permitted to preach. Pope Honorius III approved this order in 1218, which followed the rule of Augustine. The order was known as the Order of Preachers (O.P.).

Preaching was important to Dominic because he felt that it promoted love of God and love of neighbor, as Christ taught us. Although usually only ordained men were permitted to preach, Dominic convinced Church officials to approve lay persons as preachers who could move beyond the walls of the monastery, thus being more effective in missionary work. Yet this was to be a community of preachers, because Dominic believed fervently in the model portrayed in the Acts of the Apostles: a community of believers who would support each other as they evangelized. As Zagano notes, "In

Dominic's understanding, preachers were called to be the living reflection of the gospel they proclaimed. Hence for him the vows of chastity, poverty, and obedience were meant to recreate and transform the preacher into an apostle, a living witness to the crucified and risen Lord, Jesus Christ" (xv).

Dominic wrote very little. Much of what we know of him comes from other writers.

Hallmarks of Dominican Spirituality

Dominican spirituality emphasizes preaching.

Just as Christ preached, those imitating Christ should preach—all in the service of God and neighbor. Since preaching was a witness to one's faith in and love for God, it was meant to be apostolic in nature. Dominic understood how important it was to bring persons to Christ through heart-felt evangelization. Effective preaching flows from a real relationship with Christ and his gospel. Preaching, for Dominic and his followers, is not limited to formal preaching at liturgies but also includes teaching and living authentic lives of holiness.

Preaching was not to be materially profitable for the preacher. The models for Dominic's order were to be the apostles who preached not for individual gain but for the building up of the reign of God. This means that even those who are not "official" preachers in our Church can evangelize or witness the beauty of the faith to others, because we all have a role in building up God's reign. How we live preaches as forcefully as any words we might say.

Dominican spirituality emphasizes study.

Dominic believed that a good preacher must be well informed and must constantly seek the truth in order to avoid heresy. There must be both intellectual as well spiritual engagement with scripture. In terms of communal life, all Dominican houses had to have a lector in theology who would lecture daily on scripture; attendance at these lectures was required of all members of the order. Study was not pursued for one's own gain but for the sole purpose to preach more effectively. Intellectual pursuits were legitimate only if they served to help an individual grow in love (Zawilla 290).

Dominican spirituality cultivates silence and contemplation.

Dominic firmly believed that one needed silence and time to incorporate the fruits of one's study into one's relationship with God. One does not learn to love by studying alone, but rather by encountering God in prayer. For Dominic, prayer was not saying words but also listening carefully to God, especially through the Mass, scripture, and the Liturgy of the Hours, which had to be recited even when traveling for preaching purposes. Dominic believed that interior dialogue with God's word is dialogue with Christ himself.

Dominican spirituality embraces a prayer life grounded in the liturgy.

Choral participation in the Mass and the Liturgy of the Hours was required of members of Dominic's order. Yet Dominic was practical as well. There was not to be so much singing as to leave little time for study and preaching! For that reason, a Dominican chant was developed which was simpler (and less time-consuming) than liturgical Gregorian chant.

Dominican spirituality emphasizes communal life.

Adopting the rule of Augustine, but also greatly moved by the earliest Christian communities as they are described in the Acts of the Apostles, Dominic emphasized the importance of communal living. Ideally, such communities would have unanimity in their love of God and their zeal to do God's work. Yet, each community would be unique because of the unique individuals who lived together. Hence, each community developed its own customs after they had lived together for a while, as they would know what they most needed in order to live a life that was faithful to the gospel. Group discernment was practiced because Dominic believed that the group had more wisdom than any single individual. The monks prayed, ate, studied, and worked together, under the guidance of a superior. The community must be of one mind and one heart, in imitation of the Trinity; the community must be "intent on God," as St.

Augustine put it. In addition, it was the entire community's responsibility to evangelize by their word and example.

The Dominicans also borrowed from the Cistercians. Lectio divina was emphasized, as well as individual prayers. Silence was strongly encouraged in order to learn to listen to God and to others. Vows of poverty, chastity, and obedience were required. Poverty and simplicity of life was demanded—both individual and communal. Just as Christ was poor, so too should be his followers. Chastity was embraced in order to model Christ's chastity more closely. Obedience to one's superiors was modeled on Christ's obedience to his Father. Fasting and other acts of penance were encouraged to help individuals and the community as a whole to focus more sharply on God. If even greater austerity or ascetical practices were needed to keep one's mind focused on God, these were to be embraced, not for their own sake, but always to increase one's love for and union with God.

Dominican spirituality has a deep devotion to Mary.

Dominic was devoted to Mary and encouraged those who followed him to share that devotion. The Dominicans were instrumental in the development and promotion of the prayer that we know as the rosary.

Dominican spirituality encourages prayer that is incarnational.

Dominic described nine ways of prayer, some of which emphasized bodily gestures. While some of his ideas would strike modern people as masochistic (e.g., beating oneself with chains), it must be remembered that Dominic was a person of his times, and that saints of his era (and beyond) described similar practices.

To his credit, Dominic clearly understood that human beings are physical and their prayers should reflect their physicality. Hence, physical gestures such as bowing, kneeling, and extending one's arms in prayer were important, not in themselves but in the fact that they demonstrated that one's entire being was involved in prayer—body, mind, and spirit. As such, praying was a gift of one's entire self to God, a reminder that we modern people often need.

Like Dominic's monks, we do well to pray both individually and communally.

Dominican spirituality encourages a life that is a balance of contemplation and action.

For Dominic, contemplation alone was insufficient because it would fill one with love of God and love of others, but service was needed to perfect this love. Conversely, action alone was not enough because one could act without thought. Both were gifts of God. Both contemplation and service were needed in order to love. As the great Dominican Thomas Aquinas noted:

> Sometimes a person is called away from the contemplative life to the works of the active life on account of some necessity of the present life, yet not so as to be compelled to forsake contemplation altogether . . . [and here he cites Augustine]: "if it be imposed on us, we must bear it because charity demands it of us. . . ." [*de Civ. Dei* xix, 19] Hence, it is clear that when a person is called from the contemplative to the active life, this is done not by way of subtraction, but of addition. (Woods 76)

Well-Known Dominicans

Albert the Great (1206–1280): Brilliant Dominican scholar and bishop, teacher of Thomas Aquinas, and proponent of the importance of Aristotelian thought for theology.

Meister Eckhart (1260–1329): Known as the Father of German mysticism. Dominican academic who explored God's essence and the relationship between God and human beings.

Catherine of Siena (1347–1380): Italian laywoman, mystic and friend of the poor; also a peacemaker and mediator among warring factions in the Church and in her society. Was instrumental in returning the papacy to Rome after its exile in Avignon, France. Known as the "Mother" of the Dominicans.

Thomas Aquinas (1225–1273): Perhaps the Church's greatest mind ever. Because of his great love for the eucharist, he initiated the Feast of Corpus Christi and wrote several hymns, including *Pange Lingua* and *Tatum Ergo*. Wrote *Summa Theologiae*, a majestic discourse on Christianity.

In addition to his keen mind, Thomas also possessed a mystical spirit. God was totally transcendent, but Thomas believed that human beings could learn something about God in three ways: affirmations about God *(via positiva)*, what we cannot say about God given our human limitations *(via negativa),* and that which is revealed by God that goes beyond the first two ways of knowing *(via eminentiae* or way of transcendence (Woods 71). After a religious experience a short time before his death, he said, "All that I have written seems to me like straw compared to what has now been revealed to me."

References for Learning More about Dominican Spirituality

Nichols, Aidan. "Dominican Spirituality" in Stephen Costello, ed. *The Search for Spirituality: Seven Paths within the Catholic Tradition*. Dublin, Ireland: Liffey Press, 2002. 135–157.

Vidmar, John. *Praying with the Dominicans*. Mahwah, NJ: Paulist Press, 2008.

Woods, Richard. *Mysticism and Prophecy: The Dominican Tradition*. Maryknoll, NY: Orbis Books, 1998.

Zagano, Phyllis, and Thomas McGonigle. *The Dominican Tradition* (Spirituality in History Series). Collegeville, MN: Liturgical Press, 2006.

Zawilla, Ronald. "Dominican Spirituality" in Michael Downey, ed. *The New Dictionary of Catholic Spirituality*. Collegeville, MN: Liturgical Press, 1993.

six

Franciscan Spirituality

Francis and His World

One of the most beloved Catholic saints is Francis of Assisi (1182–1226), often called the holiest person in the Christian tradition other than Christ himself. He lived a radically simple life of prayer, preaching, begging, and caring for the poor and for nature. Francis founded the Order of Friars Minor, commonly known as the Franciscans. He so identified with Christ that in 1224, two years before his death, markings appeared on his hands and feet that matched the five wounds of Christ; these markings are called the stigmata.

Francis of Assisi was the son of a prominent cloth merchant and lived a carefree life in his youth, one marked by privilege and frivolity. He was popular with his peers, and from early on, Francis wanted to climb the social ladder. Originally he decided to be a knight. Accordingly, he became a soldier, but after injury, imprisonment, illness, and convalescence, his aspirations turned inward. As he evaluated the life he had been leading, he had a mystical experience, one that ultimately would lead to his renunciation of wealth and privilege.

Even though he had this mystical experience, Francis's conversion took time. But then he encountered a leper. Francis and many others of his time were frightened of lepers because the common belief was that they were highly contagious. In those days, since leprosy usually ended in death, this fear seemed reasonable. Over-coming his fear, and seeing Christ in the leper, Francis embraced the leper and experienced a deep conversion to Christ.

In 1205, while praying in the abandoned Church of San Dami-ano, he heard a voice from the crucifix urging Francis to rebuild his church. Although Francis initially thought that the church he was meant to rebuild was the physical one in which he found himself, he eventually came to realize that the voice (which Francis understood to be that of Christ) was speaking of the universal Church.

Francis resolved to live in poverty so as to be in solidarity with the world's outcasts—the poor, the ill, the powerless—and, by so doing, live in solidarity with Christ. After a time, Francis attracted followers, men who shared his view of Christian living. His initial rule of communal living was approved in 1209, and the final papal order making the Franciscan a recognized order came in 1223. Fran-cis's rule demanded that those following him would live in commu-nity, in poverty, in humility, and in conformance with the gospel.

One of Francis's followers was Clare of Assisi (1194–1253). Clare was of a noble family and could have had her choice of a number of eligible young men. She wished, however, to dedicate her life to God and refused all offers of marriage. Even in her teens, she devoted herself to the poor. When she learned about Francis, she began to follow him, seeing in him a kindred spirit. Eventu-ally Clare would found an order of female Franciscans, the Poor Clares. They too embraced poverty, believing that they were to be utterly dependent on God for everything. As such, they cared for one another's needs. Their rule was well balanced, sensitive, and compassionate.

Clare valued poverty for herself and her sisters because it was in imitation of her beloved Christ. She wrote, "God-centered pov-erty, whom the Lord Jesus Christ Who ruled and now rules heaven and earth, Who spoke and things were made, condescended to em-brace before all else" (Short 58). To her sisters, she wrote,

> O marvelous humility, O astonishing poverty! The
> King of angels, the Lord of heaven and earth, is

laid in a manger! . . . dwell on the holy humility, the blessed poverty, the untold labors and burdens which he endured for the redemption of mankind. . . . contemplate the ineffable charity which led him to suffer on the wood of the Cross and die thereon the most shameful kind of death. (Short 63)

Because Italian society of the time prevented women from living on their own, the sisters were supported by what the male Franciscans could acquire through begging. In return, the sisters taught Francis and his male followers what it meant to be lovers of Christ, joined to him by deep affection.

Hallmarks of Franciscan Spirituality

Franciscan spirituality is marked by a devotion to Christ, with a special emphasis on his humanity—Franciscan spirituality emphasizes how God humbled himself in becoming human.

All Franciscans are called to imitate the humble Christ out of love for him and gratitude to him. Francis himself was deeply moved by Christ's humility, especially his willingness to become human for us. In this incarnation, Christ was meek, obedient, and gracious. In response, we are to be the same. For Francis, Christ's mission was summed up in the "crib, cup, and cross" (Cotter 160). The humble Christ was born in a manger and laid in a crib. (As an aside, it was Francis who first created the nativity scenes around a manger in 1223 in Greccio, Italy.) Christ instituted his self-giving to us through the sharing of the bread and the cup at the Last Supper. He died an excruciating death for us on a cross.

In turn, our response to Christ should be one of loving humility, awe, and gratitude. We are to draw closer to him through frequent prayer; love for and frequent reception of the eucharist, Christ's self-gift to us; and reading of scripture, so that we will have an increasingly clearer impression of his will. We repent and do penance out of sorrow for what we have done (or failed to do) and out of love for Christ. Doing so will enable our hearts to love him more fervently and be a home for him.

When we love Christ in all things, we do what Christ would do; we are Christ to those whom we encounter. Our beliefs and our actions correspond so that we become persons of integrity.

Franciscan spirituality is marked by simplicity.

For Francis, the ultimate example of humility is the incarnation. The God who had created humanity became a human being out of love. The God who had everything surrendered it all in order to become one with his creatures. In addition, Christ comes in the humble form of bread to feed us in the eucharist.

We did not make ourselves; God made us. We did not give ourselves the gifts we have been given; God gave the gifts. Since God is the source of all we are and have, we should be grateful and humble. In short, we recognize that we are not God.

Our lives need to be simple, since many material goods can distract us from God. If that was true in Francis's time, how much truer is it today when most of us have far more than we need! Living in simplicity means that we do not take more of the world's resources than we need. We pay attention to our needs, not our wants and desires. We recognize that we are pilgrims in this world and so we should travel lightly.

Franciscan spirituality is marked by commitment to a God-centered poverty.

Francis said, "In this world, He, together with the most blessed Virgin, His mother, willed to choose poverty" (Short 43). Francis urged individual and communal poverty. Christ relied on God alone, and Franciscans were to do the same. Contrary to popular opinion, interior and exterior poverty is a sign of freedom, not deprivation. Francis understood that all creation belonged to each one of us, so there was no room for deprivation. Deprivation exists because some human beings want to exclude others from the world's goods. Thus, Francis taught that we must be in solidarity with those who have been excluded from their rightful possession and inheritance. This, too, is an imperative for us today, as we seek justice for those who are impoverished through no fault of their own or because of the dishonesty or cruelty of their leaders.

Franciscan spirituality emphasizes service and hospitality to others, especially the poor.

Franciscan spirituality reminds us that ultimately we are to respect and serve others because each person has Christ within. Like other founders of orders, Francis was very affected by Matthew 25 ("Whatever you do to the least of these, you do to me"). For that reason, he taught that we should treat others as we would treat Christ himself. Furthermore, we are to show hospitality to strangers, as Matthew 25 also makes clear. Each stranger bears the image of Christ. Each stranger is Christ himself. Thus, Franciscan spirituality is never a retreat from the world but a full engagement with it.

Franciscan spirituality reminds us of the oneness of all people.

All people—regardless of race or beliefs—are sisters and brothers in the family of God. As such, they deserve love, respect, dignity, and justice. Francis lived this belief. In 1219, he traveled to the Holy Land and met with the sultan leader of the Muslim army engaged in battle during the Fifth Crusade; actually, in order to meet the sultan, Francis went from the Crusaders' camp to the Muslim camp, accompanied only by another friar. Francis easily could have been killed by the sultan, as he openly acknowledged his faith in Christ. Instead of harming him, the sultan spoke with him, gave him a gift, and had him returned safely to the Christian camp. Because of this belief, Francis is considered the patron saint of inter-religious dialogue. How much we need his spirit today in our troubled world!

Franciscan spirituality is joyful.

Because of all the good things God has done and continues to do for us, we are called to be filled with joy. In addition, as we grow in intimacy with God, we become more joyful, reflecting God, who is joy. We demonstrate our joy by how we conduct ourselves in the world.

Francis believed in the utmost importance of prayer, through which we give ourselves to Christ and are shaped into his disciples.

Prayer is one way we can unite with God, as we speak *and* listen to God; true communication requires both. We can express sorrow to God for what we have done and for what we have failed to do, which is never-ending, since we are not perfect. As flawed human beings, we are in constant need of conversion and renewal. We are in constant need of asking ourselves "What does my heart love the most? Is it God alone?" "How do I refuse God's invitation to grow in intimacy with him?" Contrition for what we have done (or failed to do) and penance allows us to be mastered by the God of love.

Francis encouraged his friars to pray both individually and in community, especially the Liturgy of the Hours. One of Francis's first prayers for his Franciscans was, "We adore you, Lord Jesus Christ, in all, your churches throughout the world, and we bless you, for through your holy cross, you have redeemed the world." This is known as the Prayer before a Crucifix. A variant of this prayer is used during the Stations of the Cross. Although the Way of the Cross had been honored by pilgrims to the Holy Land for centuries before Francis lived, it was Francis who developed the format of the service that we now know.

Perhaps Francis's best-known prayer is the following one, which I memorized as a student in a high school under the direction of Franciscan sisters:

> Lord, make me an instrument of your peace.
> Where there is hatred, let me sow love.
> Where there is injury, pardon;
> Where there is doubt, faith;
> Where there is despair, hope;
> Where there is darkness, light;
> Where there is sadness, joy.

O Divine Master, grant that I may not so much seek
To be consoled as to console,
To be understood as to understand,
To be loved as to love.
For it is in giving that we receive,
It is in pardoning, that we are pardoned,
It is in dying that we are born to eternal life.

Like the gospel itself, this prayer reverses the ways of the world. The world insists that we look out for ourselves and our loved ones; let others take care of themselves! In the gospel and Francis's prayer of peace, we place ourselves in the subordinate position, permitting God and other persons to have the preferred position.

Franciscan life is lived in community

For Francis, communal living underscored his belief that no one person takes precedence over others. We are to be in mutual ministry to one another, for we learn what our essence is by being in relationship with others, especially during trying times.

Franciscan spirituality is both incarnational and practical

Love is nothing unless it plays itself out in life. It is not an intellectual exercise, and it is not just a "feeling." Real love is hard work, because people are not always easy to love. Real love requires humility, meekness, forgiveness, service, courtesy, and graciousness. Just as Christ did not just join us in spirit but in body as well, so, too, are we to join with our sisters and brothers in their physical, psychological, and spiritual struggles. We are to assist them in any ways that we can and which they desire. This is the message of the gospel. We are to live the gospel and love the gospel because the gospel *is* Christ. This is a foundational Franciscan belief.

Franciscan spirituality is marked by devotion to Mary.

Like other founders before him, Francis admired Mary's devotion to her Son, her obedience to God, and her faithfulness to God's plan. In this, she is a model for us as well. In Francis's world, knights were devoted to their ladies. It was the age of chivalry. As a result, Francis urged his followers to serve only one lady, Mary, to whom they were to have complete devotion. She was the way to her Son.

Franciscans recognize the goodness and oneness of all creation.

Creation is a gift from God. For Francis, concern for all creation is akin to reverence for Christ since creation bears the image of Christ. Hence, we are all related—sisters and brothers—through Christ, and, for Francis, these relationships extended to the non-human world. Francis respected the animal world, and there are many legends about Francis's abilities to communicate with animals and other forces of nature. For this reason, he is considered the patron saint of the environment. Following Francis's example today means respecting and taking care of all of creation, in whatever way we can, through measures like recycling, acquiring only what we need (and not what we want), and ending the waste of our natural resources. The Franciscan ideal also calls us to respect and care for all non-human living creatures, such as animals and plant life.

The Canticle of the Sun

This introduction to Francis concludes with another famous prayer of his: the Canticle of the Sun, in which he praises God through creation (adapted from Batten 31–33). Note that he considers even non-living forces his sisters and brothers.

> O most high, almighty, good Lord God, to Thee belong praise, honor, glory, honor, and all blessing!
>
> Praise be my Lord God with all His creatures; and specially our brother the sun, who brings us the day, and who brings us the light; fair is he, and shining with a very great splendor: O Lord, he signifies to us Thee!
>
> Praised be my Lord for our sister, the moon, and for the stars, which He has set clear and lovely in heaven.

Praised be my Lord, for our brother, the wind, and for air and cloud, calms and all weather, by which Thou uphold in life and all creatures.

Praised be my Lord for our sister, water, who is very serviceable to us, and humble, and precious, and clean.

Praised be my Lord for our brother, fire, through whom Thou give us light in the darkness; and he is bright, and pleasant, and very mighty and strong.

Praised be my Lord for our mother, the earth, which sustains and keeps us, and brings forth diverse fruits and flowers of many colors, and grass.

Praised be my Lord for all those who pardon one another for His love's sake, and who endures weakness and tribulation; blessed are they who peaceably shall endure, for Thou, O most Highest, shall give them a crown!

Praised be my Lord for our sister, the death of the body, from whom no man escapes. Woe to him who dies in mortal sin! Blessed are they who are found walking by Thy most holy will, for the second death shall have no power to do them harm.

Praise and bless the Lord, and give thanks to Him, and serve Him with great humility.

Well-Known Franciscans

St. Anthony of Padua (1191–1231): Franciscan friar, preacher, and Doctor of the Church. His talents in preaching and scholarship provided him numerous opportunities as a teacher.

St. Bonaventure (1217–1774): Franciscan friar, theologian, and Doctor of the Church. He organized Franciscan major themes into a unified spiritual-theological system.

John Duns Scotus (1266–1308): Brilliant Franciscan philosopher and teacher; author of numerous technical theological works.

Catherine of Genoa (1447–1510): Mystic, devoted to the care of the poor and ill.

Leonardo Boff (1938–): Brazilian liberation theologian, who emphasizes a sacramental view of creation.

References for Learning More about Franciscan Spirituality

Batten, J. Minton. *Selections from the Writings of St. Francis of Assisi*. Nashville, TN: The Upper Room, 1952.

Blastic, Michael. "Franciscan Spirituality" in Michael Downey, ed. *The New Dictionary of Catholic Spirituality*. Collegeville, MN: Liturgical Press, 1993.

Cotter, Francis. "Franciscan Spirituality" in Stephen Costello, ed. *The Search for Spirituality: Seven Paths within the Catholic Tradition*. Dublin, Ireland: Liffey Press, 2002. 159–190.

Short, William. *Poverty and Joy: The Franciscan Tradition*. Maryknoll, NY: Orbis Books, 1999.

"Stations of the Cross." Accessed at http://www.communityof hopeinc.org/wayofthecross/St.%20Francis%20of%20 Assisi%20Stations.html

seven

Ignatian Spirituality

Ignatius and His World

Ignatius of Loyola (1491–1556) was born into a wealthy family in Spain. In his early life, he was attracted to a career in the military; specifically, he dreamt of becoming a knight, with all the honor that was associated with that calling. While defending Pamplona against the French in 1520, he was seriously injured. During the lengthy period of recuperation, he was bored and began to read whatever was available to him. Two books made a lasting impression on him: *Golden Legend*, which was his era's "lives of the saints," and Augustine's *Confessions*. The latter work prompted an evaluation of the life he had been living thus far, and from that point on, he resolved to become a knight for Christ.

Once he had recovered from his injuries, Ignatius traveled to Montserrat, where he placed his sword at the altar dedicated to Mary, and he pledged himself to Christ. From Montserrat, he went to Manressa, where he stayed for nearly a year. This was a tumultuous year, as Ignatius experienced both spiritual highs and lows. Although he was overjoyed at the prospect of a new life, he experienced great anxiety about his worthiness. This anxiety was marked by great scrupulosity in which he was plagued by doubts that he had been forgiven for his many sins. During this time, he neglected his hygiene and his health.

Eventually, Ignatius had a number of mystical experiences that made him realize that he was loved by God. Through these mystical experiences, he received insights about God's creative activities, Christ's presence in the eucharist, Christ and his mother, and the Trinity. An additional insight that was revealed to Ignatius was that in addition to God's good spirit, there is an evil spirit that seeks to separate us from God, by making us doubt whether God loves us or whether our sins have been forgiven. Ignatius concluded that it was an evil spirit that was at work in his own doubts. These various insights will be discussed later in this chapter.

Ignatius finally acknowledged that God cared for us, and that God both desired us and wanted us to desire him in return. God's desire for us is always greater than our desire for God, but fear makes us doubt this. Once we are free of fear, we can find God, or permit ourselves to be found by God. Furthermore, God is to be found everywhere, in whatever walk of life we find ourselves. It was at Manressa that he began working on the spiritual guide that would become his *Spiritual Exercises*.

After leaving Manressa, Ignatius went to Paris to study. He studied Latin and philosophy in order to be ordained, which occurred in 1537. While a student, Ignatius was surrounded by individuals who shared his beliefs. However, as he began to share his Exercises with these like-minded individuals, he encountered difficulties with Church authorities who were concerned that he claimed to have personal revelation from God. Personal revelations were subject to suspicion in Ignatius's time. The authorities also worried that the Exercises were too affective and not sufficiently intellectual. Eventually, the authorities permitted the *Spiritual Exercises* to stand, and by 1538, Ignatius had drawn up a constitution for the men gathered about him, called the "Company of Jesus," which became the Society of Jesus (or the Jesuits) in 1540. Ignatius never set out to found an order, but he did intend to be part of a de-cloistered group that would preach the gospel.

Hallmarks of Ignatian Spirituality

Ignatian spirituality emphasizes that God loves and supports us in our efforts to get to know him.

Ignatius's mystical experiences made him realize that God was truly on the side of humanity. Furthermore, because God is relational, God desires a relationship with every person but will not force it. Unfortunately, all too often our images of God are heavily influenced by what others have told us of God or our own life experiences, as we, in effect, make God into our own image and likeness rather than let God be God. When we realize that God wants us, we should be deeply moved to want God in return.

Ignatian spirituality fosters an intimate relationship with Christ.

Like many great spiritual leaders before him, Ignatius was moved by the fact that Christ became one of us through the incarnation. Through his humanity, Christ had an intimate knowledge of what the human condition is actually like. This, for Ignatius, showed that Jesus desires an even deeper intimacy with us out of his great love for us.

Ignatian spirituality encourages external and internal poverty.

Through the incarnation, Christ experienced the poverty of the human condition. Just as Christ was poor on earth, his followers are called to be poor. Ignatius believed that this poverty is not only external, material poverty, but also recognition of one's internal poverty, i.e., that all one is and has depends on God. Christ was poor out of love for us, and we are called to be poor out of love for him.

Ignatian spirituality encourages chastity.

As Christ was chaste, his followers are called to be the same. This chastity is in thought, word, and deed. In the Examen (see below), Ignatius repeatedly made this point.

Ignatian spirituality emphasizes obedience to God and to the pope.

Ignatius understood that prayer, activity, and the vows of poverty, chastity, and obedience were all directed to God. Yet he acknowledged that the Pope was God's representative on earth and merited our respect and obedience as well.

Ignatian spirituality is communal but not cloistered.

Although the Jesuits lived in community, they were not sequestered from the world, since they saw their mission as preaching the gospel to and teaching those outside the walls of monasteries and churches.

Ignatian spirituality is marked by prayer and service.

Jesuits were called to be contemplatives in the midst of service in a very busy, noisy world, for in the world, they encountered Christ. Both attitudes were important in terms of true spiritual growth.

Ignatian spirituality emphasizes the importance of the emotions.

Ignatius believed that God created our emotions as well as our minds and souls. For that reason, our emotions could be used by God to reach us and used by us to draw closer to God. This was exemplified in the *Spiritual Exercises* when Ignatius urges the one doing the Exercises to imagine himself speaking with Christ or to imagine herself in a particular scene from the gospels. Such imaginative meditation involved the emotions as well as the intellect.

Ignatian spirituality emphasizes the importance of discernment.

At the same time, Ignatius recognized that it was important to discern the ways in which God might be trying to reach us. Ignatius points out that God can reach us with both consolations (feelings of intense intimacy with God) and desolations (a sense that God is absent or God is not present with us). Ignatius wrote:

> I call it consolation when an interior movement is
> aroused in the soul, by which it is inflamed with
> love of its Creator and Lord, and as a consequence,

can love no creature on the face of the earth for its own sake, but only in the Creator of them all. It is likewise consolation when one sheds tears because that move to the love of God, whether it be for sorrow for sins, or because of the sufferings of Christ our Lord, or for any other reason that is immediately directed to the praise and service of God. Finally, I call consolation every increase of faith, hope, and love, and all interior joy that invites and attracts to what is heavenly and to the salvation of one's soul by filling it with peace and quiet in its Creator and Lord. (#316)

I call desolation what is entirely opposite of what [was] described . . . as darkness of soul, turmoil of spirit, inclination to what is low and earthly, restlessness rising from many disturbances and temptations which lead to want of faith, want of hope, want of love. The soul is wholly slothful, tepid, sad, and separated, as it were, from its Creator and Lord. (#317)

Examples of consolations include a feeling of love or desire toward God; a sense of being at peace with God, others, and self; a sense of confidence in God and in the love of God for the world and for oneself; and an experience of inner, personal freedom. Examples of desolations include a sense of separation from God; a sense of self-disgust or self-hatred; a sense that one is at odds with God and with oneself; an inability to accept or trust in God's forgiveness; an experience of being paralyzed by fear, anxiety, attachments, addiction; an apparent inability to meet God at all (Lonsdale 97–98).

Ignatius was adamant that no major life changes should be made while one was experiencing desolation, since, at this time, the mind and spirit could not discern clearly. He was equally as adamant that while in a desolation, one should "intensify activity against desolation" (#319) and "strive to persevere in patience" (#321). On the other hand, he counseled that when one is experiencing consolation, one should remain humble, since the gift is of God and not of one's own efforts (#324).

Ignatius knew, as a result of his own trials, that we have to discern the spirits to determine which spirit is at work when we experience consolations and desolations. Ignatius was convinced that both consolations and desolations had the potential to come from spirits (or inclinations) good and evil. Although it might seem that consolations are from a good interior inclination and desolations are from an evil one, what seems to be might not always be true in actuality. Ignatius spent a good deal of time warning those who entered into his *Spiritual Exercises* that evil can masquerade as good (#331–335). Recall Ignatius's great anxiety over his sinfulness and his doubts as to whether he could ever be forgiven. He concluded that this was from evil, not from God.

Ignatius developed rules for discernment of spirits. Among them were that *all* actions must lead to the goal of our creation: the praise of God and the salvation of our souls (#169). To Ignatius, some choices are unchangeable (e.g., one's state in life), while most are changeable. "It is necessary that all matters of which we wish to make a choice be either indifferent or good in themselves, and such that they are lawful within our . . . Church, and not bad" (#170).

Ignatius's rules for making a choice are:

1. think about the matter about which one must make a choice;
2. consider the goals of creation (praising God and one's salvation) and approach the matter to be decided as neutrally or indifferently as possible;
3. ask God's guidance for what ought to be decided in this matter;
4. consider the pros and cons of the matter, weighing disadvantages against advantages;
5. prayerfully determine which alternative seems more reasonable or in keeping with the goal of creation;
6. offer the choice to God. (#178–183)

Ignatius also gave an alternative method of making a choice, one that appeals to those who benefit from using their imaginations rather than logic. In this alternative, Ignatius recommended that one imagine oneself speaking to a person one did not know to in order to help that person make the same choice; imagine oneself making the choice on one's deathbed; or imagine oneself before God on Judgment Day, reflecting on what choice one would have wished to have made (#184–187).

Ignatian spirituality utilizes the Spiritual Exercises.

The *Spiritual Exercises* can be thought of as a school of prayer (Egan 522). The purpose of the Exercises is to seek, discover, and do God's will. The Exercises have a four "week" structure, although a "week" is not necessarily seven days but is as long as it takes for a person to complete the meditations. In other words, they are to be adapted to the person making the Exercises, for the Exercises help one to determine how much he or she *really* desires God and how much time he or she *really* gives to God. It is a difficult thing to discover how little time we give to God or how little we are attached to God compared with other material objects or people. Yet, Ignatius firmly believed that one could seek God's specific will and that God would communicate directly with a devout and humble soul. But God always takes the lead and is in control.

The Exercises consist of meditations on creation and the life of Christ. Creation, which was a result of God's goodness and love, contains observable traces of this good and loving God. As such, meditating on creation was one way to come to know God. Christ became human so that God's plan for all of humanity would unfold. As such, the events of Christ's life are really our events.

It is significant that Ignatius began the *Spiritual Exercises* by a prayer attributed to him, but which was, in reality, in existence long before his birth. It is called the *Anima Christi* (Spirit of Christ), and sets the tone for the Exercises in terms of their pointing to Christ (Puhl xvii).

Soul of Christ, sanctify me.
Body of Christ, save me.
Blood of Christ, inebriate me.
Water from Christ's side, wash me.
Passion of Christ, strengthen me.
O good Jesus, hear me.
Within Thy wounds, hide me.
Permit me not to be separated from Thee.
From the wicked foe defend me.
At the hour of my death, call me.
And bid me come to Thee.
That with Thy saints I may praise Thee
Forever and ever. Amen.

The first "week" is described as the *purgative way*. The directee is encouraged to meditate on the reality of sin and its consequences. Each person has played a role in salvation history, for good or for ill. The human ability to be separated from God is because of human free will, since we can choose to love or reject God. In this first week, Ignatius introduced the Examen (also known as the examination of conscience), a prayer designed to reveal just how far we are from God, just how much we prefer ourselves to God, just how much we neglect others because we prefer ourselves. The Examen will be discussed in greater detail later in this chapter.

The second "week" is known as the *illuminative way* and focuses on Christ's incarnation, nativity, hidden life, and public life. By understanding events in Christ's life, we can better imitate him and be in solidarity with him, through poverty, forgiveness, and suffering—or whatever situations come our way.

In this second week, Ignatius introduces two standards—that of Christ and that of the evil one. Under which standard do we serve? To whom do we *really* belong? We must examine ourselves and decide; then, we must act accordingly. Ignatius warned those engaged in the Exercises that the evil one could deceive us by leading us to do something "good" for a self-serving reason.

In the third and fourth "weeks," called the *unitive way*, one experiences union with God through Christ's suffering (third week) and his resurrection (fourth week). The goal for the person making the Exercises is to be one with Christ, and by being one with Christ to be united to God. In the unitive way, one's intellect and emotions work together as the one engaged in the Exercises thinks about the realities of Christ's life and experiences them through imagination, mental images, and religious emotions. These "weeks" cannot be rushed and, ideally, should be expressed physically, emotionally, and spiritually. Through the unitive way, we get to know Christ's sorrows and joys more intimately. By learning more about Christ, we learn more about the Trinity. As we focus more on Christ, we focus less on ourselves.

Evidence that spiritual growth is occurring includes greater intimacy with God, behaving in more Christ-like ways, greater eagerness to serve others, and more generous and less self-serving motives—in short, a life that is more authentically human.

The Examen: In Ignatius's Own Words

24. First, in the morning, immediately on rising, one should resolve to guard carefully against the particular sin or defect with regard to which he seeks to correct or improve himself. 25. Secondly, after dinner, he should ask God our Lord for the grace he desires, that is, to recall how often he has fallen into the particular sin or defect, and how to avoid it for the future. . . . 26. Thirdly, after supper, he should make a second examination, going over as before each single hour, commencing with the first examination and going up to the present one.

. . . 36. There are two ways of sinning mortally [in thoughts]. The first is to consent to the evil thought with the intention of carrying it out, or of doing so if one can. 37. The second way of sinning mortally is actually carrying out the sin to which consent was given. This is a greater sin for three reasons: 1. Because of the greater duration; 2. Because of the greater intensity; 3. Because of the greater harm done to both persons.

[With regard to words] 38. (One may also offend God in word in many ways: by blasphemy, by swearing.) One must not swear, neither by the creature, nor by the Creator, unless it is according to truth, out of necessity, and with reverence. By necessity, I mean that the truth I swear to is not just some true statement I choose to confirm by oath, but one of real importance, either for the welfare of the soul or of the body, or with regard to temporal interests. By reverence I mean that when the name of the Creator and Lord is mentioned, one acts with consideration and devoutly manifests due honor and respect. 39. It must be noted that in idle oaths we sin more grievously when we swear by the Creator than when we swear by a creature. . . .

40. (Among other sins of the tongue that we must avoid are idle words.) No idle words should be uttered. I understand a word to be idle when it serves no good purpose, either for myself or another, and was not intended to do so. . . . 41. (Lying, false testimony, detraction are also sins of the tongue.) Nothing should lessen the good name of another, or to complain about him. For if I reveal a hidden mortal sin of another, I sin mortally; if I reveal a hidden venial sin, I sin venially; if his defect, I manifest my own. . . . (Among sins of the tongue may be considered ridicule, insults, and other similar sins. . . .)

[With regard to deeds] 42. The subject matter for examination will be the Ten Commandments, the laws of the Church, the recommendations of superiors. All transgressions arising from any of these three groups are more or less grievous sins, according to the gravity of the matter.

Method of Making the General Examination of Conscience. There are five points to this method. 1. The first point is to give thanks to God our Lord for the favors received. 2. The second point is to ask for grace to know my sins and to rid myself of them. 3. The third point is to demand an account of my soul from the time of rising up to the present examination. I should go over one hour after another, one period after another. The thoughts should be examined first, then the words, and finally, the deed in the same order as was [previously] explained. . . . 4. The fourth point will be to ask pardon of God our Lord for my faults. 5. The fifth point will be to resolve to amend with the grace of God. Close with an *Our Father.* (Puhl 15–23)

Well-Known Jesuits

Gerard Manley Hopkins (1844–1889): Noted English poet whose works have Christian themes, e.g., the beauty of creation, the incarnation.

Pierre Teilhard de Chardin (1881–1955): French paleontologist and theologian who synthesized science and theology in an original—and sometimes controversial—fashion, with all creation converging to an "omega point" which is Christ.

Karl Rahner (1904–1984): German priest who was a theological advisor to the Second Vatican Council. His theology focused on the human person and God's presence in each human life.

References for Learning More about Ignatian Spirituality

Egan, Harvey. "Ignatian Spirituality" in Michael Downey, ed. *The New Dictionary of Catholic Spirituality*. Collegeville, MN: Liturgical Press, 1993.

Lonsdale David. *Eyes to See, Ears to Hear: An Introduction to Ignatian Spirituality*. Maryknoll, NY: Orbis Books, 2000.

Mottola, Anthony, trans. *The Spiritual Exercises of Saint Ignatius: St. Ignatius' Profound Precepts of Mystical Theology*. New York: Image Books, 1989.

Puhl, Louis. *The Spiritual Exercises of St. Ignatius: Based on Studies in the Language of the Autograph*. Chicago: Loyola Press, 1951.

Veale, Joseph. "Ignatian Spirituality" in Stephen Costello, ed. *The Search for Spirituality: Seven Paths within the Catholic Tradition*. Dublin: Liffey Press, 2002.

eight

Salesian Spirituality

Francis de Sales, Jane Francis de Chantal, and Their World

Francis de Sales (1567–1622) was born in France, the firstborn child of loving parents who provided him with a Jesuit education. Although he was intellectually stimulated by the rigorous education that he received, his understanding of Augustine's and Aquinas's views on predestination deeply troubled him. Because Francis himself had been so surrounded by love in his family and had taken delight in those books of scripture that described God's love for human beings, he firmly believed that God would extend grace, love, and mercy to all, but that each person needed to accept these gifts.

Through his Jesuit education, he was exposed to the spiritual exercises of Ignatius. As a student, he developed his own, more practical version on how to get himself through the day. He imagined what might occur in a given day, including any difficulties, and sought God's will in his day, thereby offering the day to God. Naturally, Francis's day included Mass, prayer, and service, but it also included "sacred sleep," a time that he would meditate on God's love and goodness. This student work was expanded and, many years later, was eventually published as *Introduction to the Devout Life*. It was a text that he used in spiritual direction for both ordained and lay persons.

Francis became a priest, initially doing missionary work in Protestant territories. Later, he became Bishop of Geneva, but he never lost his focus on the love of God and love of human beings. Even as bishop, he served others, especially acting as a confessor to many, clergy and laity alike. Francis had a gift for mediation and used this gift in both religious and secular arenas. He saw his work in mediation as areas of concrete service to God, the Church, and the people for whom he worked tirelessly.

In addition to founding an order for men with one of his directees, Jane Francis de Chantal (1572–1641), he founded the Visitation Nuns of Holy Mary, named after Mary's visitation of her cousin Elizabeth. Jane was a widow when she first met Bishop de Sales. She expressed her desire to give herself to God. Together, they developed a flexible religious community for women, especially for those who were not candidates for traditional convents: older or disabled women, and women with family duties. The flexibility would permit them to take care of personal or family duties in a way that honored who they were but still enabled them to serve God and their neighbors. Such communities emphasized mutual love, concern, humility, gentleness, and trust. The sisters were to devote themselves to God through prayer and gentle service, both marked by patience and love.

Jane's beliefs about the importance of love of God are well summarized in the following passage, comments made aloud to her sisters and recorded by her secretary:

> My dear daughters, Saint Basil and most of the fathers and pillars of the Church were not martyred. Why do you think that is? . . . For myself, I believe that there is a martyrdom called the martyrdom of love in which God preserves the lives of his servants so that they might work for his glory. This makes them martyrs and confessors at the same time. I know . . . that this is the martyrdom to which the Daughters of the Visitation are called and which God will allow them to suffer if they

are fortunate enough to wish for it. . . . What happens . . . is that divine love thrusts its sword into the most intimate and secret parts of the soul and separates us from our very selves. I know one soul . . . whom love had severed in this way who felt it more keenly than if a tyrant with his sword separated her body from her soul [she was speaking of herself]. . . . [how long might this martyrdom last] From the moment . . . when we have given ourselves up unreservedly to God until the moment we die. But this is intended for generous hearts who, without holding themselves back, are faithful in love. Hearts that are weak and capable of only a little love and constancy are not martyred by Our Lord. He is content to let them go on in their little way so they won't fall by the wayside. God never violates free will. . . . martyrs of love suffer a thousand times more by staying alive to do God's will than if they had to give a thousand lives in witness of their faith, love, and fidelity. (Wright 64–65)

Clearly, Jane was in tune with Francis's idea of a "world of hearts." Francis believed in the importance of loving friendships, especially spiritual friendships with both men and women. Because the Trinity is relational, and God is relational with human beings, relationships are important in spiritual growth.

Don Bosco was born the son of peasants near Turin, Italy, in 1815. His father died when he was very young, and he grew up in very modest circumstances. For this reason, he always had a great concern for poor and working-class youth. After his ordination to the priesthood in 1841, he began to work with the poor, homeless, and neglected boys of Turin, a ministry he had envisioned since his youth. Specifically, his dream was to help these boys understand that they had an intrinsic worth that society could not take from them, and he would instill this understanding through gentle treatment of the boys.

He began this calling by acquiring houses where homeless and vulnerable boys could get shelter and receive an education. In doing this, he had to face many obstacles, as many individuals did not want these youth in their neighborhoods, a theme that is all too often heard today. Bosco's work was also hindered by individuals inside the Church, but he persevered.

In 1859, Bosco founded the Pious Society of St. Francis de Sales, or Salesians. He chose St. Francis de Sales as the Society's patron, in part because Francis had been known for his gentleness and agreeable nature, even in the midst of religious and political obstacles. In words that could have been written today, Bosco had this to say about youth.

> The young constitute the most fragile yet most vulnerable component of human society. . . . They are not of themselves depraved. Were it not for parental neglect, idleness, mixing in bad company, something they experience especially on Sundays and holy days, it would be so easy to inculcate in their young hearts moral and religious principles. . . . For if they are found to have been ruined at that young age, it will have been due more to thoughtlessness than to ingrained malice. These young people have real need of some kind of person who will care for them, work with them, guide them in virtue, keep them away from evil. . . . (Wright 123–24)

Hallmarks of Salesian Spirituality

Salesian spirituality calls us to "live Jesus."

Francis believed that we should imitate Jesus in everything we do. Such imitation demonstrates our love for him, for to "live Jesus" is to have his name always on our hearts. We are to incorporate the heart of Jesus into our own hearts in order to heal the world. Francis disagreed with the notion that one had to leave the world—be sequestered in a monastery—in order to find God. There is no need to leave the world, for Christ is to be found precisely *in* the world. Hence, one can live Jesus wherever one is and whatever one is doing. Francis, a great proponent of using one's imagination, would encourage people to pray by placing oneself in God's presence, simultaneously becoming increasingly aware of God's presence everywhere. No matter who we are, we must let Christ enter every situation and relationship; Francis understood that it was only by Christ's living in human hearts that they could be healed and transformed. Christ's indwelling leads us to God, no matter what vocation one has.

Salesian spirituality is epitomized by "A World of Hearts."

The incarnation of Christ is the story of love. All was created for Christ. Thus, the heart of God, the heart of Christ, and the heart of humanity are joined. Because God is love, and, therefore, the source of human love, when we act with love, God is present. Although the human ability to love is seriously marred by sin, Christ heals us of our sinfulness—if we are willing to be healed. In this healing, we are again reunited to God in love. When we surrender ourselves to Christ, his own gentleness and humility can become ours. We can truly love one another, which is the vocation of all Christians.

As an aside, both Francis and Jane had a great devotion to the Sacred Heart of Jesus and the heart of his mother. In fact, the emblem of the Visitation nuns are two hearts superimposed on one another, both pierced and surrounded by a crown of thorns.

Salesian spirituality emphasizes love of the Trinity.

Francis saw the Trinity as relational, as all three Persons love each other with an infinite love. Furthermore, the Persons wish to include every human person in their love; that is why human beings were created. In this way, to use the words of Wright, the human heart "is made to beat in rhythm with the heart of God" (33). Jesus came as the mediator between the divine heart and the human heart because "human hearts are 'arrhythmic'; they . . . beat to a rhythm of their own. They are not at one with the heart of God. They are wounded or tarnished through original sin" (33).

Salesian spirituality seeks union with God.

Francis believed that God loves and wants each one of us. Union with God could be realized anywhere and in any walk of life; one did not have to be a mystic! In other words, God calls us wherever we are—in the loftiest of positions as well as in the poorest of states. As long as we sincerely desire to draw closer to God, union will occur. Humility is important because we need to recognize our complete dependence on God and be willing to obey God in everything we do. We are not God. Our ability to remain humble and obedient is cultivated by prayer, the sacraments, spiritual direction, and loving service for others. In this way, our union with God becomes increasingly closer.

Salesian spirituality acknowledges human relationships as a window to God.

Both Francis and Jane recognized that human relationships draw us closer to God. In this, they were excellent models themselves. We respect and love others because God dwells in them as well as dwells in us. In relationship, we are called to respect others' freedom even as God respects ours. As our union with God increases, as we live Jesus more faithfully, our ability to love others will mature, not just others whom we know well, but all with whom we come into contact. When this happens, we are less interested in our schemes and plans, and more invested in others' lives. This leads to our treating others with genuine respect, gentleness, graciousness, and loving service. We treat others as if they are one of a kind . . . which they are. We start to see with God's eyes.

Salesian spirituality understands that there is a universal call to holiness.

Holiness is not reserved for vowed religious and the ordained. It is the vocation of every man, woman, and child, regardless of his or her station in life. This should bring us all great joy! Prayer, the sacraments, and service are available to everyone. Francis was a firm believer in this idea and made this point vigorously in his *Introduction to the Devout Life*. From that work, here are Francis's questions about how we relate to God, others, and ourselves:

How does your heart stand toward God himself? God should be at the top of your desires and aspirations. When lovers are separated, how they long for each other! How often they are on each other's thoughts and imagination. When they are together, how they fill each other's lives. So should we strive to have the love of God enlighten our heart. . . . Can you discover any sacrifices you have made for the love of God? Anything you have given up for him? True love shows itself in deeds as well as words. (Chapter V:4, "On the State of the Soul towards God")

How do you love yourself? Do you love this earth so much you want to make a great name for yourself and live always here? . . . Do you observe due order in self-love? Inordinate love of self ruins us while a well-ordered love puts soul ahead of body, virtue ahead of honors, and eternal values beyond temporal ones. Be more interested in what the angels and saints may think of you, rather than what men would say. . . . Consider yourself as God looks at you. Humility should come easily here. It consists not in esteeming self above others and in not desiring to be esteemed by others. Do you sometimes boast of yourself, or flatter yourself? Consider your language. Do you sometimes put pleasure before duty? Do you sometimes risk your health through food, drink, or lack of sleep? (V:5, "A Spiritual Look at Ourselves")

The love between husband and wife should be sweet and tranquil, constant and persevering, because God wills it and orders it. The same is true for love of our children, relatives, and friends, each according to rank. But examine yourself in a general way, too. How are you disposed toward your neighbor? Do you try to love with your whole heart for love of God? Test yourself by thinking of someone who is troublesome or disagreeable. We certainly exercise love of God toward our neighbor if we can be well-disposed toward those who injure us or harm us by word or deed. Take a reasoned look at how you are apt to speak of your neighbors, especially those who dislike you. (V:6, "How We Consider Our Neighbor")

Another Well-Known Salesian

Margaret Mary Alacoque (1647–1690): A sister whose mystical encounters with Christ led to the Nine First Fridays devotion. Demonstrating the Salesian devotion to hearts of love, Margaret Mary wrote:

This divine heart is an inexhaustible fountain from which three streams are continually flowing. The first is the stream of mercy, which flows down upon sinners and brings the spirit of sorrow and repentance. The second is the stream of charity which brings relief to all those who are suffering under some need, and especially those who are striving for perfection. . . . The third is the stream of love and light for perfect friends whom He wills to unite with Himself. Moreover, this divine heart will be a sure refuge and a harbor of safety at the hour of death for all those who have honored it during life. It will protect and defend them. (Wright 102)

References for Learning More about Salesian Spirituality

Chorpenning, Joseph. "Salesian Spirituality" in Michael Downey, ed. *The New Dictionary of Catholic Spirituality.* Collegeville, MN: Liturgical Press, 1993.

Francis de Sales. *Introduction to the Devout Life.* Charles Dollen, ed. New York: Alba House, 1992.

Wright, Wendy. *Heart Speaks to Heart: The Salesian Tradition.* Maryknoll, NY: Orbis Books, 2004.

nine

Lay Spirituality

Not only are the ordained called to holiness and a deeper relationship with God; laypersons are as well. Most of the founders of the various spiritual movements described in this book recognized that. Yet, a separate lay spirituality reinforces the idea that all are called to Christian discipleship, achieving this through their particular everyday activities. There is, however, no one specific founder of "lay" spirituality.

While having a deep respect for their community elders, the earliest Christians did not distinguish between their leaders and the rest of the community in the same way we do today. Christ himself was a "layman," to use modern terms. He was not a Jewish priest; in fact, he often criticized the recognized religious leaders of his time. The early Church believed that every baptized person had a role, for all were called to imitate Christ in his compassion, hospitality, and inclusiveness. After the third century, *laikos* ("laity") was the term used to describe the non-ordained. Yet, there still remained an understanding that there was a priesthood of all believers.

Unfortunately, recognition that each Christian was a member of the priesthood of all believers diminished over time. In the twentieth century, both lay and ordained theologians and other Christian leaders began to reclaim the teaching of the universal call to holiness.

To be sure, many Church reforms throughout history were led by laypersons, especially women. Notable examples are Julian of

Norwich, Teresa of Avila, and Catherine of Siena. Lay movements that arose in the twelfth to thirteenth centuries embraced a simple lifestyle, ordinary work, and communities of friends—all in imitation of Christ.

As laypersons became better educated, they assumed greater roles in the Church, especially in our own time. Like their ordained counterparts, laypersons meditated daily, sought spiritual direction, and took part in the Church's liturgies, sometimes daily.

It was the Second Vatican Council (1962–1965) that emphasized the universal call to holiness and the necessity of the gifts of every person, clergy and laity, since both together comprise the people of God and share in Christ's priestly, royal, and prophetic roles. Clergy and laity must collaborate with each other rather than compete with each other, as each have their own spheres of influence and both are necessary in the body of Christ.

The Council highlighted the laity in two of its documents. In *Lumen Gentium*, the Council's vision of the Church, the bishops had this to say:

> But by reason of their special vocation, it belongs to the laity to seek the kingdom of God by engaging in temporal affairs and directing them according to God's will. They live in the world, that is, they are engaged in each and every work and business of the earth and in the ordinary circumstances of social and family life which, as it were, constitute their very existence. There they are called by God that, being led by the spirit to the Gospel, they may contribute to the sanctification of the world; as from within like leaven, by fulfilling their own particular duties. Thus, especially by the witness of their life, resplendent in faith, hope, and charity, they must manifest Christ to others. It pertains to them in a special way so to illuminate and order all temporal things with which they are so closely associated that these may be effected and grow

according to Christ and may be to the glory of the
Creator and Redeemer. (LG 31)

In addition to *Lumen Gentium,* the Council provided an entire document on the laity, *Apostolicam Actuositatem* (Decree on
the Apostolate of the Laity). Noting that modern conditions require
that the laity's apostolate be "broadened and intensified" (#1) the
Church fathers affirmed that "the laity likewise share in the priestly, prophetic, and royal office of Christ and therefore have their
own share in the mission of the whole people of God in the Church
and in the world" (#2). "The laity derive the right and duty to the
apostolate from their union with Christ the head: incorporated into
Christ's Mystical Body through Baptism and strengthened by the
power of the Holy Spirit through Confirmation, they are assigned
to the apostolate by the Lord himself. . . . The sacraments, however,
especially the most holy Eucharist, communicate and nourish that
charity which is the soul of the entire apostolate" (#3). Each person
has the "right and duty" to use his or her God-given charisms "in
the Church and in the world for the good of men and the building
up of the Church" (#3).

Laypersons are called to be faithful witnesses to Christ in their
families, in their workplaces, in social outreach, and in their local
parishes. In short, laypersons are called to transform the world. The
bishops realized that laypersons would have to be prepared for their
roles. In chapter six of *Apostolicam Actuositatem*, they encouraged
lives of prayer; frequent reception of the sacraments (especially the
eucharist); spiritual formation; healthy human relationships, including those with people not of the Christian faith; a "solid doctrinal
instruction in theology, ethics, and philosophy adjusted to age, sta-
tus, and natural talents" (#29); small Christian communities; and
the like. Furthermore, preparation for evangelization and sanctification should begin in the home, as parents and the Church (through
local pastors) pass on to children and teens the riches of the faith.

How do laypersons better live the faith so as to transform the
world? *Apostolicam Actuositatem* continues:

There are many aids for laypersons devoted to the apostolate, namely, study sessions, congresses, periods of recollection, spiritual exercises, frequent meetings, conferences, books, and periodicals directed toward the acquisition of a deeper knowledge of sacred Scripture and Catholic doctrine, the nourishment of spiritual life, the discernment of world conditions, and the discovery and development of suitable methods. (#32)

Many of the major orders discussed in this book welcome laypeople into their orders. In addition, there are newer lay movements in the Church, such as the Cursillo movement.

Hallmarks of Lay Spirituality

Because of its emphasis on bringing the gospel to the world, lay spirituality must balance prayer and action, obedience and freedom, and care for creation in the midst of technological advances. Authentic Christian lay spirituality integrates our experiences with scripture, the sacraments and liturgies, and Christian community so that we are not only prepared but also energized to share this "good news" with the world.

Lay spirituality emphasizes love for God and for others.

We love God by loving others. When we love others, we serve them and want justice for them, regardless of where they live or who they are. We are called to participate in this unselfish love, the same love Christ had for us. Although this sounds simple, it is difficult to consistently love others as they are, i.e., to love as Christ loves us. For example, do we strive to love relatives and others around us with whom we disagree or with whom we do not easily get along? Our neighbors? Our coworkers?

Lay spirituality assumes an active prayer life.

Without a daily, intentional connection to God, spiritual growth simply does not occur. Although most laypersons cannot adhere to the strict schedule of prayer as those in monasteries or convents might, they are called to devote some part of each day to communication with God, ideally first thing in the morning, last thing at night, and occasionally during the day. Laypersons can pray in the ways that they find most helpful—whether by standard prayers or by just "talking" with God.

Lay spirituality flourishes with frequent attendance at Mass and frequent reception of the sacraments.

The Mass is the Church's majestic communal prayer in which we join with Christ. Daily attendance permits one to better appreciate the universality of the Church and the fact that we are all united in Christ. In addition, frequent reception of eucharist and the sacrament of reconciliation is spiritually edifying. Sharing in the body and blood of Christ provides food for life's journey, providing strength for the times when the going gets rough. Frequent confession is also necessary for spiritual growth. It brings us to the reality that we have many flaws that get in our way. We are sinful. Yet, in spite of this sinfulness, God is always ready to extend forgiveness to us. Although some people wonder why they cannot confess directly to God (they can and should), instead of to another human being, confession to a priest is both a joyful and a humbling experience. It can remind us of the incarnation (when Christ humbled himself by choosing to become human) and provide us with the Church's assurance that we are forgiven by the power invested in the Church by Christ himself.

Lay spirituality becomes better developed through sacred reading.

Frequent reading of scripture familiarizes us with the story of our salvation. If read in a *lectio divina* fashion, the scripture "reads us," as we recognize ourselves in the characters of scripture and get a better sense of where God is calling us in our own lives. Devotional reading of other texts important in our Catholic tradition is also recommended, although such texts should not take the place of scripture. As with prayer, we need to make time in our lives for sacred reading.

Lay spirituality encourages sharing one's faith with others, especially participation in a small Christian community.

We were not meant to be alone, and participation in a small Christian community reminds us of this. We can learn from the faith journey experiences of others. We hear other persons' ways of praying, their interpretation of scripture, and incorporation of Christian beliefs into their daily lives. We hear how others have made time for spiritual disciplines in their lives. We come to appreciate God's call to each person. Almost every parish has small Christian communities who welcome new members or who are willing to help establish new communities. We do well to participate in such groups for both our benefit and that of others.

Lay spirituality involves intentionally learning more about our faith.

Unfortunately, some adults have not learned anything new about their faith since their confirmation classes. This is tragic. The Church's treasury is so great that there is always more to learn. In humility, we can take advantage of the opportunities to learn more—through parish adult education offerings; through diocesan-wide seminars or workshops; and through classes or courses of study offered by schools of theology. Although there are many on-line courses, these should be used sparingly, since there is indeed great benefit in being with other students in the same room.

Lay spirituality grows stronger with spiritual guidance.

At one time, spiritual guidance was felt to be necessary for only the ordained or vowed religious. That is no longer the case. We can all have a spiritual friend or companion, someone who is our peer with whom we can pray and share our spiritual insights, joys, doubts, fears, and questions. We can also have a spiritual guide, someone who has some training in the spiritual life, someone who can guide us during our times of joy as well as in our times of distress or doubt, by offering helpful advice based on sound principles. We can have a spiritual director, someone who has special training in spiritual development over the course of a lifetime and how psychological development affects spiritual development (and vice-versa). Names of spiritual guides or directors can be obtained from local retreat houses or from the diocesan office.

But keep in mind that the true spiritual director is the Holy Spirit. The human beings to whom we go keep us accountable for progress in the spiritual life. After all, it is too easy to fool ourselves if we fail to share with another person. At times, we are too easy on ourselves, while at other times we are too hard. We need another person who loves God and cares about our spiritual progress to keep us on track.

Lay spirituality is marked by service to others.

Throughout this book, we have learned that the spiritual founders of specific schools of spirituality firmly believed that spiritual growth is impossible without service to others. If we are to be our authentic selves, the persons whom God created us to be, we must live concretely the beliefs we profess. We serve others because they are children in God's family, our sisters and brothers, as dearly loved by God as we are. We serve others because Christ did so in his earthly ministry. We serve others because we love them, as Christ instructed us to do.

Well-Known Lay Spiritual Practitioners

So many could be named! But for our purposes, especially in our troubled economic and political times, and in light of the immediately preceding section on service, an excellent example is Dorothy Day (1897–1980). Day's early life was not in keeping with Christ. Yet, after a conversion experience, she became a champion of gospel values of non-violence, poverty, and solidarity with the poor. She co-founded the Catholic Worker Movement (CWM), dedicated to workers but also to the poor. As part of her ministry, she wrote articles in a newsletter published by the CWM.

Here are excerpts from several issues of the CWM newsletter.

From "Room for Christ," December 1945:

> It is no use to say that we are born two thousand years too late to give room to Christ. Nor will those who live at the end of the world have been born too late. Christ is always with us, always asking for room in our hearts.
>
> But now it is with the voice of our contemporaries that he speaks, with the eyes of store clerks, factory workers, and children that he gazes; with the hands of office workers, slum dwellers and suburban housewives that he gives. It is with the feet of soldiers and tramps that he walks, and with the heart of anyone in need that he longs for shelter. And giving shelter or food to anyone who asks for it, or needs it, is giving it to Christ. . . .
>
> If we hadn't got Christ's own words for it, it would seem raving lunacy to believe that if I offer a bed and food and hospitality for Christmas — or any other time, for that matter — to some man, woman, or child . . . my guest is Christ. . . .
>
> It would be foolish to pretend that it is easy always to remember this. If everyone were holy and handsome, with "alter Christus" shining in neon lighting from them it would be easy to see Christ in everyone. . . .
>
> We are not born too late. We can do it [i.e., make up for the neglect by the many] by seeing Christ and serving Christ with friends and strangers, in everyone we come in contact with. . . . All of our life is bound up with other people; for almost all of us happiness and unhappiness are conditioned by our relationship with other people. What a simplification of life it would be if we forced ourselves to see that everywhere we go is Christ, wearing

out socks we have to darn, eating the food we have to cook, laughing with us, silent with us, sleeping with us. . . .

It is not a duty to help Christ, it is a privilege.

From "Look Upon the Face of Christ," July-August 1947:
The first time I saw a bread line with its homeless ones, footsore, wrapped in rags, my heart turned over within me. "You have wounded my heart, my love," Jesus Christ himself said. "I have no place to lay my head." . . . And what if it is their own fault, these poor? What about the story of the Prodigal Son? How the Father loved him and welcomed him! We can only show our love for Christ by our love for these his least ones.

From "To Die for Love," September 1948:
If we cannot deny the *self* in us, kill the self love, as He has commanded, and out on the Christ life, then God will do it for us. We must become like Him. Love must go through purgations. . . .

It is hard to believe in this love [God's love for us] because it is a devouring love. It is a terrible thing to fall into the hands of a living God. If we do once catch a glimpse of it, we are afraid of it. . . .

That most people in America look upon love as an illusion would seem to be evidenced by the many divorces we see today — and the sensuality of despair that exists all around us. But all these divorces may too be an evidence about love. They hear very little of it in this war-torn world, and they are all seeking it. Pascal said of love, "You would not seek me if you had not already found me." . . .

One wants tenderness, not pity, respect and friendship and not clinging, doting love. A doting love is an oppressive love; and one sees it in the love of parent for child, and in the love of one partner for the other. One revolts from such a love. One wants to . . . escape from such slavery, such serfdom.

But true love is delicate and kind, full of gentle perception and understanding, full of beauty and grace, full of joy unutterable. . . . And there should be some flavor of this in all our love for others. We are all one. We are one flesh, in the Mystical Body, as man and woman are said to be one flesh in marriage. With such a love, one would see all things new, we would begin to see people as they really are, as God sees them.

Much hospitality could be given to relieve the grave suffering today. But people are afraid. They do not know where it all will end. . . . No use starting something you cannot finish, they say. . . . We don't want to pay the cost of love. We do not want to exercise our capacity to love.

References for Learning More about Lay Spirituality

Apostolicam Actuositatem (Decree on the Apostolate of the Laity). Accessed at http://www.vatican.va/archive/hist_councils/ii_ vatican_council/documents/vatii_decree_19651118_apostolicam -actuositatem_en.html.

Day, Dorothy. "Look Upon the Face of Christ." *The Catholic Worker*, July-August 1947. Doc. #457. Accessed at www.catholicworker .org/dorothyday/index.cfm.

_____. "Room for Christ." *The Catholic Worker*, December 1945. Doc. #416. Accessed at www.catholicworker.org/ dorothyday/index.cfm.

_____. "To Die for Love." *The Catholic Worker*, September 1948. Doc. #470. Accessed at www.catholicworker.org/dorothyday/index.cfm.

Lumen Gentium (Dogmatic Constitution on the Church). Accessed at www.ignatiusinsight.com/features2006/colson_rolelaity1_oct06.asp.

Sellner, Edward. "Lay Spirituality" in Michael Downey, ed. *The New Dictionary of Catholic Spirituality*. Collegeville, MN: Liturgical Press, 1993.

ten

Mystical Spirituality

The term "mystical spirituality" describes a form of consciousness of the divine that goes beyond ordinary experience. A person
having such a mystical encounter or union with God feels like he
or she is encountering reality for the first time; what seemed to be
hidden or belonging only to God is now revealed. This enlightenment through union with God leads to the ultimate purpose of mystical spirituality: an increasingly fervent love of God and others,
and a deep reverence toward God, other persons, and all creation.
In Christian belief, one can experience the hidden Christ in scripture or in the eucharist; these experiences change a person who then
lives accordingly.

Like lay spirituality, mystical spirituality has no "founder."
Mystical experiences are reported in the Old Testament (e.g., Mo-
ses and the burning bush) and in the New Testament (e.g., the trans-
figuration of Jesus). Mystical experiences are reported in the sacred
texts of other world religions as well. Many Christian saints have
spoken of mystical experiences: Paul, Augustine, Gregory of Nys-
sa, Bernard of Clairvaux, Teresa of Avila, Ignatius of Loyola, and
John of the Cross, to name just a few. In fact, when Teresa spoke
of the "Prayer of the Quiet," she was referring to a mystical experience. Even modern writers such as Thomas Merton, Evelyn Under-
hill, and Karl Rahner speak of mystical experiences.

There are no special techniques to practice in order to have a
mystical experience, since mystics believe that the experiences are

pure gift from God who is beyond all knowing. As the mystical part of the prayer increases, the human being does less and less, as God does more and more.

Experiences such as visions and auditions (i.e., voices) are sometimes associated with mystical experiences, but not always. The same is true of ecstasies, in which one has a sense of being outside oneself, immersed in Love itself.

In his work *What Is Contemplation?* Merton had this to say about mystical prayer in his own, inimical fashion. It is so on target that a large section is quoted here:

> It would be a great mistake to think that mystical contemplation necessarily brings with it a whole litany of weird phenomena—ecstasies, raptures, stigmata, and so on. These belong to a quite a different order of things. . . . Infused contemplation . . . is deep and intimate knowledge of God by a union of love—a union in which we learn things about Him that those who have not received such a gift will never discover until they enter heaven. Therefore, if anyone should ask, "Who may desire this gift and pray for it?" the answer is obvious: *everybody*. But there is only one condition. If you desire intimate union with God, you must be willing to pay the price for it. . . .
>
> The fact remains that contemplation will not be given to those who willfully remain at a distance from God, who confine their interior life to a few routine exercises of piety and a few external acts of worship and service performed as a matter of duty. Such people are careful to avoid sin. They respect God as a Master. But their heart does not belong to Him. They are not really interested in Him, except in order to insure themselves against losing heaven and going to hell. In actual practice, their minds and hearts are taken up with their own

ambitions and troubles and comforts and pleasures and all their worldly interests and anxieties and fears. God is only invited to enter this charmed circle to smooth out difficulties and to dispense rewards. (8–12)

Do not therefore lament when your prayer is empty of all precise, rational knowledge of God and when you cannot seize Him any longer by clear, definite concepts. Do not be surprised or alarmed when your will no longer finds sweetness or consolation in the things of God and when your imagination is darkened and thrown into disorder. You are out of your depth; . . . This is precisely as God wants it to be, for He Himself is that object and He is now beginning to infuse into the soul His own Light and His own Love in one general, confused experience of mute attraction and powerful desire. Do not seek anything more precise than this for the moment. If you attempt by your own action to increase the precision of your knowledge of God or to intensify the feeling of love, you will interfere with His work, and He will withdraw His light and His grace, leaving you with the fruit of your own poor natural activity. (59–60)

In mystical spirituality, God can be encountered in terms of what God is, as well as what God is not. Two Greek words have been used traditionally to describe these two ways of understanding God. *Kataphatic* refers to knowledge about God that describes God's attributes, while *apophatic* refers to knowledge about God that describes God in terms of what God is not.

Because it is pure gift from God, there are no techniques to mystical spirituality. In addition, it is difficult to note hallmarks of this spirituality because the experiences of the mystics are so varied. After all, God works with each person individually. For that reason, let us hear from the mystics themselves. In the following passages, they describe kataphatic experiences (in terms of something that could be described) or apophatic experiences, which are beyond human understanding or experience, so that there are no words to faithfully describe it.

Examples of Kataphatic Experiences

St. Paul: 2 Corinthians 12:1–4

> I knew a man in Christ above fourteen years ago, (whether in the body, I cannot tell; or whether out of the body, I cannot tell; God knows) such as one caught up to the third heaven. And I knew such a man (whether in the body, or out of the body, I cannot tell; God knows). How that he was caught up into paradise, and heard unspeakable words, which is not lawful for a man to utter.

Julian of Norwich: Showings

> He also showed me a little thing, the size of a hazelnut, lying in the palm of my hand. It was as round as a ball, as it seemed to me. I looked at it with the eyes of my understanding and thought, "What can this be?" My question was answered in general terms in this fashion: "It is everything that is made." I marveled how this could be, for it seemed to me that it might suddenly fall into nothingness, it was so small. An answer for this was given to my understanding: "It lasts, and ever shall last, because God loves it. And in this fashion, all things have their being by the grace of God." In this little thing, I saw three properties. The first is God made it. The second is that God loves it. The third is that God keeps it. . . . It is necessary for us to know the littleness of creatures . . . so that we may love

and have the uncreated God . . . the only real rest.
(chapter 5, 183)

Richard Rolle: The Fire of Love

> O honeyed flame, sweeter than all sweet, delightful
> beyond all creation!
> My God, my Love, surge over me, pierce me by
> your love, wound me with your beauty.
> Surge over me, I say, who am longing for your
> comfort.
> Reveal your healing medicine to your poor lover.
> See, my one desire is for you; it is you my heart is
> seeking.
> My soul pants for you; my whole being is athirst
> for you.
> Yet you will not show yourself to me; you look
> away;
> You bar the door, shun me, pass me over;
> You even laugh at my innocent sufferings.
> And yet, you snatch your lovers away from all
> earthly things.
> You lift them above every desire for worldly
> matters.
> You make them capable of loving you — and love
> you they do indeed.
> So they offer you their praise in spiritual song
> which bursts out from that inner fire;
> They know in truth the sweetness of the dart of
> love.
> Ah, eternal and most lovable of all joys, you raise
> us from the very depths,
> And entrance us with the sight of divine majesty
> so often!
> Come into me, Beloved!
> All ever I had I have given up for you;

I have spurned all that was to be mine,
That you might make your home in my heart, and
    I your comfort.
Do not forsake me now, smitten with such great
    longing,
Whose consuming desire is to be amongst those
    who love you.
Grant me to love you, to rest in you.
That in your kingdom I may be worthy to appear
    before you, world without end. (52–53)

Teresa of Avila: The Life of Teresa of Jesus

Rapture . . . often comes like a strong swift impulse, before your thought can forewarn you of it or you can do anything to help yourself; you see this cloud, or this powerful eagle, rising and bearing you up with it on its wings . . . we must . . . go willingly wherever we are carried away, for we are in fact being carried away whether we like it or no. . . . Occasionally I have been able to make some resistance, but at the cost of great exhaustion, for I would feel as weary afterwards as though I had been fighting with a powerful giant. At other times, resistance has been impossible: my soul has been borne away, and indeed as a rule, my head also, without my being able to prevent it; sometimes my whole body has been affected, to the point of being raised up from the ground. . . .

When I tried to resist these raptures, it seemed that I was being lifted up by a force beneath my feet so powerful that I know nothing to which I can compare it, for it came with a much greater vehemence than any other spiritual experience, and I felt that I was being ground to powder. . . .

I confess that in me it produced great fear—at first a terrible fear. One sees one's body being lifted up from the ground; and although the spirit draws it after itself, one does not lose consciousness—at least, I myself have had sufficient to enable me to realize that I was being lifted up. . . .

This favor also leaves a strange detachment. . . . Although these produce a complete detachment of spirit, in this favor the Lord is pleased that it should be shared by the very body, and it will thus experience a new estrangement from things of earth, which makes life much more distressing. (190–192)

Examples of Apophatic Experiences

Meister Eckhart

If you want to be without sin and perfect, don't chatter about God. Nor should you (seek to) understand anything about God, for God is above all understanding. . . . So, if you understand anything of Him, that is not He, and by understanding anything of Him you fall into misunderstanding, and from this misunderstanding, you fall into brutishness, for whatever in creatures is uncomprehending is brutish. So, if you don't want to become brutish, understand nothing of God, the unutterable. (Woods 84)

Indeed, if a man thinks he will get more of God by meditation, by devotion, by ecstasies, or by special infusion of grace than by the fireside or in the stable, that is nothing but taking God, wrapping a cloak around His head and shoving Him under a bench. For whoever seeks God in a special way gets the way and misses God, who lies hidden in it. But whoever seeks God without any special way

gets Him as He is in Himself, and that man lives
with the Son, and he is life itself. (Woods 87)

Author Unknown: The Cloud of Unknowing

[God's] will is that you should look at him, and
let him have his way. . . . If you are willing to do
this, you need only to lay hold upon God humbly in
prayer, and he will soon help you. . . . God is ready
when you are, and is waiting for you. But what am
I to do, you say and how am I to "lay hold"? (chapter 2, 60–61)

Lift your heart to God with humble love; and
mean God himself, and not what you get out of
him. . . . Try to forget all created things that he ever
made, and the purpose behind them, so that your
thoughts and longing do not turn or reach out to
them either in general or in particular. Let them go,
and pay no attention to them. It is the work of the
soul that pleases God the most. . . . Do not give up
then, but work away at it till you have this longing.
When you first begin, you will find only darkness,
and as it were a cloud of unknowing. You don't
know what this means except that in your will, you
feel a simple steadfast intention reaching out toward God. Do what you will, this darkness and this
cloud remain between you and God, and stop you
both from seeing him in the clear light of rational
understanding, and from experiencing his loving
sweetness in your affection. Reconcile yourself to
wait in this darkness as long as is necessary, but
still go on longing after him whom you love. For if
you are to feel him, or to see him in this life, it must
always be in this cloud, in this darkness. (chapter
3, 61–62)

[God] cannot be comprehended by our intellect. . . . For we . . . are created beings. But only to our intellect is he incomprehensible; not to our love. . . . to the intellect, God is forever unknowable, but to the second, to love, he is completely knowable, and that by every separate individual. . . . (chapter 4, 63)

For whoever . . . thinks that it is fundamentally an activity of the mind, and then proceeds to work it all out along these lines, is quite on the wrong track. He manufactures an experience that is neither spiritual nor physical. He is dangerously misled and . . . unless God in his great goodness intervenes with a miracle of mercy and makes him stop . . . he will . . . suffer some other dreadful form of spiritual mischief and devilish deceit. (chapter 4, 65–66)

Do not think that because I call it a "darkness" or a "cloud," it is the sort of cloud that you see in the sky, or the kind of darkness you know at home when the light is out. . . . By "darkness" I mean "a lack of knowing"—just as anything that you do not know or may have forgotten may be said to be "dark" to you, for you cannot see it with your inward eye. For this reason, it is called "a cloud . . . of unknowing," a cloud of unknowing between you and your God. (chapter 4, 66)

If ever you are to come to this cloud and live and work in it, as I suggest, then just as this cloud of unknowing is as it were above you, between you and God, so you must also put a cloud of forgetting beneath you and all creation. We are apt to think that we are very far from God because of this cloud of unknowing between us and him, but surely it would be more correct to say that we are much farther from him if there is no cloud of forgetting between us and the whole created world. (chapter 5, 66)

Pseudo-Dionysius: Mystical Theology

Trinity! Higher than any being, any divinity, any
goodness! Guide of Christians, in the wisdom of
heaven! Lead us up beyond unknowing and light,
up to the farthest, highest peak of mystic Scripture,
where the mysteries of God's Word lie simple, absolute and unchangeable in the brilliant darkness
of a hidden silence. Amid the deepest shadow, they
pour overwhelming light on what is most manifest.
Amid the wholly unsensed and unseen, they completely fill our sightless minds with treasures beyond all beauty. (chapter 1, 135)

The fact is that the more we take flight upward,
the more our words are confined to the ideas we are
capable of forming; so that now as we plunge into
that darkness which is beyond intellect, we shall
find ourselves not simply running short of words
but actually speechless and unknowing. (chapter 3,
139)

The Cause of all is above all and is not inexis-
tent, lifeless, speechless, mindless. It is not a material body, and hence had neither shape nor form,
quality, quantity, or weight. It is not in any place and
can neither be seen nor be touched. It is neither per-
ceived nor is it perceptible. It . . . is overwhelmed
by no earthly passion. It is not powerless. . . . It
endures no deprivation or flight. It passes through
no change, decay, division, loss, no ebb and flow,
nothing of which the senses may be aware. None of
all this can either be identified with it nor attributed
to it. (chapter 4, 140–41)

Again, as we climb higher, we say this. It is not
soul or mind, nor does it possess imagination, conviction, speech, or understanding. Nor is it speech
per se, understanding per se. It cannot be spoken

of and it cannot be grasped by understanding. It is not number or order, greatness or smallness, equality or inequality, similarity or dissimilarity. It is not immovable, moving, or at rest. It has no power, it is not power, nor is it light. It does not live nor is it life. It is not a substance, nor is it eternity or time. It cannot be grasped by understanding, since it is neither knowledge nor truth. It is not kingship. It is not wisdom. It is neither one nor oneness, divinity nor goodness. Nor is it a spirit, in the sense in which we understand that term. It is not sonship or fatherhood, and it is nothing known to us or to any other being. It falls neither within the predicate of non-being nor of being. Existing beings do not know it as it actually is. . . . There is no speaking of it, nor name nor knowledge of it. Darkness and light, error and truth—it is none of these. It is beyond assertion and denial. We make assertions and denials of what is next to it, but never of it, for it is both beyond every assertion, being the perfect and unique cause of all things, and, by virtue of its pre-eminently simple and absolute nature, free of every limitation, beyond every limitation, it is also beyond every denial. (Chapter 5, 141)

References for Learning More about Mystical Theology

Julian of Norwich. *Showings* (Classics of Western Spirituality Series). New York: Paulist Press, 1978.

Merton, Thomas. *What Is Contemplation?* Springfield, IL: Templegate Publishers, 1981.

Pseudo-Dionysius. *The Complete Works* (Classics of Western Spirituality Series). New York: Paulist Press, 1987.

Rolle, Richard. *The Fire of Love*. Clifton Wolters, trans. New York: Penguin, 1972.

Teresa of Avila. *The Life of Teresa of Jesus*. New York: Image
Books, 1991.

Wiseman, James. "Mysticism" in Michael Downey, ed. *The New
Dictionary of Catholic Spirituality*. Collegeville, MN: Liturgical Press, 1993.

Wolters, Clifton, trans. *The Cloud of Unknowing*. New York: Penguin, 1978.

Woods, Richard. *Mysticism and Prophecy: The Dominican Tradition*. Maryknoll, NY: Orbis Books, 1998.

Conclusion

Now that you've learned a bit about the different major Catholic spiritual traditions, you might be saying, "So what's next?" In part, the answer depends on whether you found a particular tradition in which you are interested. If you did, you can try the following. First, read an entire work by the founder or a prominent member of that spiritual tradition. For most of these traditions, just a small portion of one of their works was included in this book to illustrate that spiritual tradition's focus. You can get a much better idea of the vision of the spiritual tradition by reading an entire book.

Within each chapter, I have also offered the names of a few of these books. Your local Catholic or Christian bookstore will have a greater selection of books on Catholic spiritualities and will be very willing to suggest additional books of interest. Because the works described in this book are classics, most bookdealers will be very familiar with them. Alternatively, you could use a search engine (like Google) to locate a particular author in order to determine whether there is a book that you would like to read.

Another way of exploring, in greater depth, a spiritual tradition in which you are interested is to attend a presentation by someone of that tradition, especially if the presentation highlights the main points of the tradition. You can find listings of such presentations in your church bulletin, a diocesan newspaper, or electronic bulletin. Many of these presentations happen at a sponsoring church or at a sponsoring diocesan event, making them easy to locate. A good thing about an on-site presentation is that it gives you a chance to ask questions and delve more deeply than you might do while just reading a book on your own.

Another option would be to attend a retreat given by a member of the spiritual tradition you find attractive. This is optimal if the retreat is held at a retreat center affiliated with that spiritual tradition. In this way, the ambiance of the building, the entire *milieu*, as it were, will wrap itself around that spiritual tradition. But even if it doesn't happen at such a place, a retreat given by someone of that spiritual tradition will undoubtedly highlight some of that tradition's hallmarks. A retreat is a fine way to get a feel for the intellectual and affective aspects of a tradition through the presentations, which appeal to the intellect, and through prayer and other rituals, which appeal to the affective sense or emotions. You can learn about retreat offerings though your church bulletin, through the diocesan newspaper or electronic bulletin, or by calling a retreat center to learn about upcoming programs or to get on their mailing list. You can get a list of retreat centers by calling the diocesan office in the city in which you live or looking up retreat centers in the yellow pages of the phone book. You can also speak to your pastor to see if he has any contacts in the spiritual tradition in which you are interested. Word of mouth is a wonderful way to find contacts, and your pastor may have several. Such contacts would be good because they would give you a chance to meet with someone and to discuss that tradition one-on-one.

But what happens if you did not find a particular tradition that inspired you, or if you were interested in several, or even all, that were presented? How would you learn more about the traditions presented here or about traditions not presented in this book? A good way to do this is by reading an anthology or collection of works by a variety of spiritual writers describing their traditions. There are many fine anthologies available at Catholic and Christian bookstores, and even at some of the larger, secular bookstore chains. In addition, sometimes one can get a calendar that has a passage from a spiritual writer for each day of the year. Anthologies, and even the calendars, contain a wealth of information and representative writings from numerous traditions. Reading a representative sample from a particular tradition might encourage you to explore a whole work by a member of that tradition, something which you can do on your own time, at your own leisure. It is important that this not become just another job to be done, but that you approach it as something which will benefit *you*. Yes, it requires a commitment of time, seemingly impossible when you already have too many things to fill that time already. Yet the payback for making that commitment can be great.

When you read a selection from a calendar or an anthology, you might find it helpful to read it in a lectio divina fashion. Although lectio was presented earlier in this book, it bears repeating at this point, since I am encouraging you to read a small amount of spiritual text each day.

First, bring yourself to silence so that you can really make space in your mind for what you are reading. Secondly, read the passage slowly and for meaning; you're not in a race, and if you really feel as if you're in a rush, perhaps you can read a little less each day, or you can carve out another piece of time (at a different time of the day) to commit to reading. Then, meditate on what you have read, thinking about the words, the situation described, and the message that seems to be obvious. You might even imagine yourself as one of the characters in a story, or even a member of the crowd who is listening to Jesus, for example. For some people, this imaginative, mental prayer is very helpful, and for others it's a complete turn-off. If it works for you, please try it. After meditating on that work, ask God to give you whatever God chooses to give through the reading of this text and ask that you be open to that gift. This prayer is followed by a period of silence, waiting for whatever wisdom or enlightenment that God chooses to give, on God's time. Then, perhaps you move to the final step, which is putting what you read into action.

For example, if you read about Jesus feeding five thousand people, it might inspire you to volunteer one morning a month at a local soup kitchen. Or, if you read a passage from Dorothy Day and get a keen sense of how she saw Christ in others, you might put yourself in that position by intentionally encountering others who are different than you, endeavoring to see Christ in all of your brothers and sisters.

Reading an anthology, or even a calendar, is an excellent way to practice the discipline of spiritual reading, as each day you read something different. And the beauty of it is that it's not always familiar. Sometimes when we read scripture, it is so familiar to us that we say to ourselves, "All right, I know this already. Yeah, let me skip through this." That's not going to happen with daily spiritual reading. Unless you are familiar with 365 days of passages, or you are familiar with an entire anthology, what you read, on most days, is going to be new to you, a surprise. God may very well use a reading to take you by surprise, to touch you where you least expect it.

If you have not found a tradition with which you resonate among the ones I have included in this book, you might talk to your pastor and ask him to suggest some readings or an anthology that he has found helpful, or to provide you with the name of someone who might give you such guidance.

I would caution you about one technological advance that may not always work to your benefit. Many people decide that they are going to explore a spiritual tradition by searching the Internet. There are a number of reputable sites on the Internet that present information about Catholic spirituality in general or the different traditions of Catholic spirituality, but there are also some very individual, opinionated sites that are not necessarily going to provide you with what you are seeking. Sometimes, individuals develop their own blogs, in which they talk about what *they* think that someone else said, or why *they* don't agree with Francis of Assisi or Francis de Sales. That's not really what you want. You want to be introduced to the tradition itself, through the home page of a religious order or a reputable Catholic site that gives you information that can be verified. Many of my students have tried to do papers for me based on the Internet, and what they have given me does not always merit a passing grade, because it is not accurate or because it is someone saying something about what someone else said about a spiritual tradition. In other words, it's three or four times removed from the actual tradition.

As I have emphasized, a spiritual tradition combines beliefs and writings with action, and sometimes a good way to see a spiritual tradition in action is to serve at one of its ministries. Many Franciscan, Jesuit, and Salesian volunteer opportunities are available, especially in work with the poor or in education. If Franciscan spirituality appeals to you and you see something going on at the local Franciscan center, perhaps you should check it out. If Jesuit spirituality really resonates with you and you see a group of Jesuit volunteers working to beautify a neighborhood, perhaps you should investigate what they do. Your local diocesan office can give you information on such opportunities or you can always look for these online. In doing so, I would suggest that you would put your city as one word in an advanced search and then say, "Jesuit volunteer opportunities," or "Salesian volunteer opportunities." In that way, you have a chance of getting information that has a greater likelihood of being accurate.

But before showing up at a ministry, *always* call ahead of time. You really do want to know what you're getting into. Unfortunately, there are charlatans all around, some of whom can sometimes take the name of a true charity, a true spiritual tradition, and twist it around so that it seems that you are working for that tradition, when you really are not.

As all the spiritual tradition founders have said, it is not sufficient to say what you believe; you've got to live it out. Volunteering on behalf of one of the great spiritual traditions—serving in a soup kitchen, tutoring children after school, visiting the sick, visiting the imprisoned—may give you a better sense of that spiritual tradition than you could get from a hundred books. In fact, it is common that individuals find the spiritual traditions that best resonate with them by getting involved with a service opportunity sponsored by these traditions. The service opportunity that seems to be the best fit for a person might help him or her to encounter that spiritual tradition. But unless the service is tied to a spiritual tradition, it is only a volunteer endeavor. There's nothing wrong with volunteerism, but when we're talking about a spiritual practice, it needs to be connected to God, because God is the focus of a spiritual practice. Volunteerism is wonderful, but a spiritual discipline and a spiritual practice are far more than volunteerism.

That is why the service associated with a spiritual tradition fits with the entire ethos of the tradition. If the tradition was founded to educate young people, that's probably where its service is going to be located. If the tradition was founded to help the poor and the needy, that's probably where its service opportunities will abound. In other words, these service opportunities are not just add-ons, but they are integral to the spiritual tradition.

It's important to realize that what's right for you might not be what's right for your best friend or for your spouse. This can be difficult because many of us like to do things with those closest to us. "Oh, come on, help me serve down at the soup kitchen," or "Come on, help me tutor the kids after school." But we have all been given different gifts. Your spouse or your best friend might not share the gift that you have been given. And so, although it is important to do things with other people, don't feel like you're a failure if you cannot get your spouse to do the service with you. Don't feel like your friendship is in jeopardy if your best friend says, "I think I'll pass on that." God calls us in unique ways, and God will call your friend or your spouse in the way that best suits him or her.

In the end, this is all about integrity. We are to be persons of integrity. What we believe must fit in with who we are and how we conduct ourselves. A spiritual tradition is not like a dress or a suit that one tries on in the store. One can't just put it on, the way different people have tried it on, to see if it's going to fit. For example, one person who practices Franciscan spirituality may practice it a little differently from another. For those who love nature, Franciscan spirituality's emphasis on creation and the environment may really hook them, but for those who don't like to be outdoors—don't have anything against creation but don't like to be outdoors—that's not going to be the major thrust. So, be who you are. Do what seems right. Do not be led against your will to do things that do not seem right.

Yet, do not be afraid of trying something new, especially if you're with someone whom you trust. Many times, spiritual growth results when God pulls us out of our comfort zones. For some of us, God gently calls us out of our comfort zones, but for many of us, God has to *pull* on us because we like being comfortable. We know what we like; we like where we are. We don't want to rock the boat; we don't want to change things too much. That's fine in some areas of life, but one never grows spiritually if one stays in the same place. In fact, one might regress a bit, because in the area of spirituality, if one is not moving forward, one is falling backward. It is often difficult to do something that seems at odds with what one has always done.

A friend of mine became involved in prison ministry. This man is an upright citizen, and he had never even received so much as a speeding ticket. The idea of a prison was abhorrent to him, as were the people who populated prisons. He was invited to get involved in this ministry, to try it, just one time. He was sure he wasn't going to like it; in fact, he was pretty confident that he was going to hate it. But he made the promise that he would go once. One visit helped him realize that he had found his calling. He met a group of inmates who really wanted to learn more about God, who really wanted to hear what God had done in other people's lives, who really wanted to hear that God was going to be there to forgive them, and who really wanted this man to minister to them. The man who had never broken the law was welcomed by the inmates, who considered him as part of their own. They looked forward to his visits, and now, several years later, he can't even imagine giving up this ministry. It has helped him grow in his own faith. That is my parting piece of advice for you.

Any spiritual tradition, any service, any prayer, must help you move closer to God, if it is authentic. Sometimes we try something and it seems to move us backward. Other times we try something, as my friend did, and it moves us closer. We are not in control. God is. Practicing a spiritual tradition sends us this message loudly and clearly. We have to be willing to be open to hearing that message, and in hearing that message, we have to be willing to act. Let us trust in God, even when it seems foolish to do so. For the wisdom of the world is foolishness to God, and the wisdom of God seems foolish to the world.

Pat Fosarelli is a theologian, physician, and lay minister. She teaches spirituality and practical theology at the Ecumenical Institute of Theology at St. Mary's Seminary in Baltimore, Maryland, and is on the part-time faculty in the Department of Pediatrics at the Johns Hopkins University School of Medicine. She has authored several books, including *The Family Ministry Desk Reference*. A recipient of multiple teaching awards, Dr. Fosarelli frequently addresses both lay and religious audiences.

Founded in 1865, Ave Maria Press,
a ministry of the Congregation of
Holy Cross, is a Catholic publishing
company that serves the spiritual and
formative needs of the Church and its
schools, institutions, and ministers;
Christian individuals and families; and
others seeking spiritual nourishment.

———◆———

For a complete listing of titles from

Ave Maria Press

Sorin Books

Forest of Peace

Christian Classics

visit www.avemariapress.com

ave maria press® / Notre Dame, IN 46556
A Ministry of the Indiana Province of Holy Cross